The Mike Hall

HOW WELSH RUGBY NEARLY CHANGED FOREVER AND CARDIFF CITY REACHED THE PREMIER LEAGUE Story

with Hamish Stuart

y Lolfa

CANOLFAN CANSER
VELINDRE
CANCER CENTRE
Codi Arian

Proceeds of this book will help provide support,
care and research at Velindre Cancer Centre

First impression: 2014

© Copyright Mike Hall and Y Lolfa Cyf., 2014

The publishers wish to acknowledge the support of
Cyngor Llyfrau Cymru

Cover design: Y Lolfa
Cover photograph: Jon Pountney

ISBN: 978 184771 710 8

Published and printed in Wales
on paper from well-maintained forests by
Y Lolfa Cyf., Talybont, Ceredigion SY24 5HE
website www.ylolfa.com
e-mail ylolfa@ylolfa.com
tel 01970 832 304
fax 832 782

Contents

Foreword

A LOT OF former rugby players have come together to raise awareness of the great work carried out at Velindre Hospital. We have all been touched by cancer in some way, so we have all tried to assist a charity which helps so much with the tragedy in people's lives.

Mike and I, along with loads of other people, have done a couple of fundraising bike rides in America, also some dinners and events to raise funds and increase awareness. We help to raise the money for Velindre and then they choose the best way to spend it.

Since I have been president of fundraising, we have raised £13 million in five years, which is an extraordinary amount of money in Wales and an incredible testament to the generosity of the people of Wales. There is not the same amount of money here as some other parts of the world, but the people are just as generous as any. That is thanks to the patrons, ambassadors and the general public, we are all part of a big team. I would also like to give a big thank you to the fundraising team and the staff at Velindre.

The bike rides in America have been incredibly rewarding. We tend not to do too much training before going, so it is a bit of a slog. However we need to do it and just get through the whole thing somehow – it is a bit like pre-season training I suppose!

We might be slightly more used to doing that than Joe Public, thanks to our rugby backgrounds, but we try to create an environment where everyone is mucking in together. It is not a race so everyone is helping each other out.

Everyone was shattered in the evenings, but we would have

some food and a couple of beers and then just head off again in the morning. People would wonder how the rugby boys did it, but the cause of Velindre cancer care puts everything into perspective.

I have known Mike for around 25 years, since he first came into the Wales squad in 1988. He was a youngster coming up from Cambridge University, a bit wet behind the ears, while I was one of the established players at that stage. He had character and determination which needed to be channelled a little in the early days, but he has done extremely well in rugby and in life. He went on to be captain of Cardiff and Wales.

In 1989 I was captain of Wales for the tour to New Zealand, where Mike won his first cap. We shared a room together on what was a very trying trip. He was in the Wales team when I went north to Rugby League later that year, then he was captain of Cardiff when I came back to Rugby Union for the Blue and Blacks and Wales in 1995. He was one of the constants in Welsh rugby over that time when so many things changed.

The last 25 years has certainly been a rollercoaster, with plenty of stories and I still consider Mike a good friend of mine over all that time.

> Jonathan Davies MBE,
> former Wales rugby captain,
> BBC pundit and President of Velindre Fundraising
> November 2014

Introduction

It is 2015 and Cardiff City are running out at their rundown Ninian Park home in League Two, battling back from bankruptcy and relegation in front of a crowd of 4,800 – pretty good for them these days. A decade before there had been big talk for Wales's capital club, but they collapsed as those grand plans plunged them into debt and administration. The enforced points deduction saw them plummet down through the leagues, the big dreams turned into nightmares.

Meanwhile at the Millennium Stadium, Sam Warburton, Jamie Roberts and Dan Lydiate are turning out for Cardiff against Toulouse in the European Rugby Super League in front of a crowd of 20,000 and a global TV audience. All the top Welsh stars play for just two professional rugby teams in Wales, both taking part in the worldwide competition dubbed 'Rugby's Packer Circus'. Adam Jones, Alun Wyn Jones and George North are playing for Swansea, the only other professional Welsh side, against Leicester at the Liberty Stadium. Below those two elite teams the traditional club game is still strong in Wales, involving all the best players outside the Wales international squad. Wales play in the Six Nations, but a unified season round the world also means greater competition with the southern hemisphere at club and international level.

With the benefit of hindsight these may seem crazy ideas as instead Cardiff City had a season alongside Swansea City in football's Premier League spotlight, thanks to their superb new stadium and sell-out crowds. Meanwhile the four Welsh rugby regions compete in Celtic and European competitions, beset by bickering within Wales and internationally, with crowds rarely topping 10,000. So this may sound like a time-travelling episode of the Cardiff-filmed *Doctor Who* television drama, but how close did the alternative scenario get to being the current day reality?

The answer is about ten minutes in the case of Cardiff City and a few days in the case of Welsh rugby. Given that they are two of the biggest stories in the history of two very different sports, amazingly one man was central to both and played a significant part in seeing Welsh sporting history take the path it has.

Mike Hall is a former captain of the Cardiff and Wales rugby teams, a British and Irish Lions Test player, who went on to become a director of Cardiff City Football Club during some of the club's most turbulent times. As a player and businessman he became heavily involved in two of the most dramatic tales that have shaped the current look of sport in Wales. This is the story of how it all happened.

* * *

Cardiff City chairman Sam Hammam dreamed of the new stadium that would awaken the capital of Wales from being the perennial sleeping giant of Welsh and British football. If Hammam was an ambitious schemer then neither he nor his motives were fully trusted by many of the people who had the power to make or break those dreams. He had made a lot of money out of Wimbledon Football Club's fairytale journey, taking them from nowhere to the top division and an FA Cup triumph, but his departure from the London side saw the club fall down the leagues, lose their home ground and move to Milton Keynes. That track record inspired both excitement and concern.

Hall and business partner Paul Guy were the men with the property experience to make Hammam's dreams a reality by putting in place the retail park that could help fund the building of a new stadium. The elephant in the room was that distrust of Hammam which meant the necessary money would only flow if he could be persuaded or forced to hand over the reins. Hammam had complete control of Cardiff City, only he could decide to pull out and it was a multi-million pound decision.

In October 2006, Hammam turned up for a meeting at the Ninian Park ground he owned at 10am. Paul Guy and Mike Hall were there to see him. Hammam faced a tough ultimatum, knowing the club faced huge debts. He was told investors were in place to save the club, but those promises of money depended on Hammam agreeing to quit before a deadline of midday. Debt-ridden Cardiff City were 120 minutes from certain bankruptcy with the clock ticking down, the administrators were already in place to take over.

The Lebanese businessman was always a battler with a particularly strong reputation for fighting hardest when backed into a corner. He refused to sign away his stake in Cardiff City, the club he considered his own, and left the ground before 10.30am. There was another 90 minutes before the deadline, but apparently no hope of a solution – even though the alternative was financial disaster for everyone involved. With no new funding and no new ground, Cardiff City faced total debts of more than £30 million. The taxman was circling, crowds were low, playing standards were slipping and it seemed the gamble to try and raise the Bluebirds to fly high in the Premier League had gone spectacularly wrong.

Administration would have been certain, resulting in an automatic points deduction and likely tumble down the leagues. The economic collapse of 2008 would have put paid to any thoughts of a new ground and brighter future at Cardiff City for a generation or more. As the clock ticked closer to midday with no sign of a deal from Hammam, the idea of Cardiff City ever playing in the Premier League seemed a million years away.

In his disappointment at Hammam's refusal to sign there and then, Hall went to the gym. There seemed nothing else to do. Years of work by the former Wales rugby captain and plenty of others to put the funding in place, working towards the retail park on one side and a state-of-the-art stadium on the other, seemed to be lying dead on the altar of one man's ego. For a sportsman like Hall, working up a sweat on the exercise machines seemed the only way of taking out his frustration with the most stubborn and difficult man he had ever dealt with...

Eleven years earlier, during the last days of amateur Rugby Union, Mike Hall had sat in a hotel room in Cardiff, surrounded by almost all of Wales' top international rugby players as they agreed to sign up to join a new professional 'circus'.

Rugby was technically an amateur game in those days, though just after the 1995 Rugby World Cup that was an ever-increasing sham. Forces backed by Australian media tycoon Kerry Packer wanted to create a rugby equivalent of cricket's Packer Circus, a rebel World Series tournament with the top players from every major rugby country. The southern hemisphere's top stars such as All Blacks captain Sean Fitzpatrick and Springboks skipper Francois Pienaar had already committed themselves in theory and now the northern hemisphere's big names were being asked to follow.

The moves were understandably Top Secret, all the deals done behind very firmly closed doors with the contracts stored in locked safes round the world. Rugby's 'Omerta', the sporting version of the Mafia's infamous vow of silence and denial, that had covered up illegal payments in the amateur era also helped to cover up the moves towards professionalism. Publicising the discussions would have meant professionalising all the top international players and alerting the game's governors. Around 50 Wales players signed contracts which were kept in a safe ready for the day they would be needed, but it all remained hushed up – until now.

Wales were to get two teams based in the largest cities, one in Cardiff and the other in Swansea. They would take part in a European Super League with a small number of clubs from each of the Five Nations countries, the English and French clubs signed up as the driving forces. The players would have been 'leased back' to the Unions for international matches in return for the new Super League being able to use the national grounds for their matches – Twickenham, Lansdowne Road, Murrayfield, Parc des Princes and of course the National Stadium at Cardiff Arms Park, before the Millennium Stadium was built.

This was at a time when amateur rugby players were expected to reach professional standards without being paid or – more importantly – being given the time necessary to hit those heights of fitness, strength and power. They were expected to hold down full-time jobs without missing training, while taking unpaid leave for internationals and tours. The gulf with the southern hemisphere, where there was greater freedom, grew wider on a daily basis.

The major threat was Wales players going to Rugby League and being lost to Union forever; this Packer plan would have seen them being paid while remaining in the international Union ranks. Amateur Rugby Union, the traditional rivalries of Welsh club rugby, would remain healthy below that elite level.

The Welsh players were approached through Wales and Cardiff captain Hall, with a similar scenario being played out in all the other major rugby-playing countries. All bar one of the Wales squad signed up and those contracts were locked in a Cardiff law firm's safe ready for the day when they would establish Rugby Union's new order.

At the time the International Rugby Board had astute Welsh lawyer Vernon Pugh as their chairman, someone who knew Hall well and was happy to ring up his captain to check the rumours of what was going on. Hall was equally happy to pass on those details and reveal their extent and depth. Pugh was then instrumental in Rugby Union going professional a few weeks later as the proposed 'Packer Circus' collapsed.

Wales entered the professional world with a host of clubs, gradually whittling down the numbers to four regions. Even now there are those who suggest that four is too many for the standard and number of players, while the traditional club level is not as strong or well supported. Who is to say how it would have turned out with just two elite professional teams in Wales, but there is certainly an argument it would have been a better way forward.

There may be ambiguity over whether rugby was better or worse off by avoiding the Packer Circus, but there is little doubt that Cardiff City have gone from strength to strength thanks to the new stadium.

There are a lot of stories for Mike Hall to tell, along with the inside track on some fascinating characters – and that is just the start of the controversy.

Hamish Stuart
November 2014

Part 1

1

Say Hello to Uncle Sam

WHEN I WAS captain of Cardiff RFC and a member of the business community in the capital city through the 90s, I would not have been surprised to be told that one day I would become a director of one of Cardiff's major sports clubs. Naturally I would have assumed that club would be Cardiff RFC, or what became the Blues. I would have been shocked then, and maybe even now, by the idea that I would end up on the Board of Cardiff City Football Club through some of the most interesting times in their history.

The very first time I got involved with Cardiff City, I was an agent working with small property advisory company Steepholm. A few of us had started the business when I was given an ultimatum that I could either stay in my previous job or go on a Wales rugby tour – but not both. We began doing some work for Cardiff-based property developer Paul Guy, who was also a director of Cardiff City, and became aware of the proposed new Cardiff City Stadium around 2003 – and in particular the retail park opportunity that was a key part of the development plans.

Samir Hammam was the Lebanese owner of Cardiff City. He was a well known figure thanks to a successful time as the owner of Wimbledon Football Club that had ended in controversy. However meeting him was very different to the reputation.

I think Sam was trying to build the retail park and the stadium himself, but he did not have the wherewithal to do it alone. Cardiff City football club could not fund a new stadium, nor could Hammam, but the retail park was expected to make a profit and some of that would be used to fund the new football stadium. Future Cardiff City chairman Peter Ridsdale told the High Court in 2008 that Sam had tried initially to use his own company Rudgwick as the developer, so profits would have gone to him rather than the football club. However it was council-owned land, Cardiff council were being careful and Hammam needed other options. I became involved as an agent because he started searching for a business partner to develop the retail park.

One of my first meetings with Hammam was when I brought Robert Ware from MEPC, a massive property company in London, down to Cardiff to meet him. Robert was a well-respected, experienced property developer and I will never forget that first meeting because Hammam was really quite rude to him. Sam had a strange way of dealing with things, swearing in the meeting. He told XXX jokes which were really inappropriate. I don't know if he was nervous or trying to impress, but it backfired spectacularly. That relationship was doomed to fail, even before it started.

Sam Hammam liked to be the one who decided what had been said or decided at meetings. We had a meeting around that time at the offices of HMA, the architects, with around 20 people in the room. We were talking about the ways the retail park would sit alongside the stadium, how the whole development would fit together. We were discussing the size of the units and the specifics that potential retailers would be looking for. Naturally I was writing down all the relevant details that I would need to talk to those retailers. Sam looked up and said: 'What are you ******* doing?' He told me to put my pen down. Of course everyone was a bit in awe of him in those early days, I was a lot younger and I was shocked. It was an important deal for our company Steepholm if we could get it so I did not want to fall out with him.

He said: 'No notes, no ******* notes.' The hackles went up on the back of my neck wondering what he was on about. How were we going to document all this without writing down in meetings what we had discussed and agreed? His secrecy in business meant that everything had to be done through him. He wanted to keep things close to his chest, but also to take the credit for everything. That was his mantra – I do not know if it was cultural differences because of his Lebanese background or just his own personality, but it was a habit of his that would have huge ramifications for everyone involved.

There was another meeting in London with Andrew Lewis-Pratt, a Welshman who was chief executive on the retail side for specialist out-of-town-developers Capital and Regional PLC. They had expertise in this area, one of their previous projects was the retail park alongside the Liberty Stadium development that houses Swansea City and the Ospreys.

Capital and Regional (C&R) were looking at the Cardiff development; the capital's football club were in dire straits and needed cash. I remember Sam absolutely banging the table, hammering on it saying: 'Just give me the ******* money.' He was very vociferous, very aggressive. He was doing that to someone who was the chief executive of a quoted property company, who could not just sign a large cheque because some football chairman was demanding it.

Depending on the circumstances he could be charming in meetings, or he could be totally volatile, you never really knew which way he was going to be. I went to a meeting with him when Rodney Berman, the openly homosexual Liberal-Democrat leader of Cardiff council, had just announced he was about to go into a civil partnership with his boyfriend. We were sitting in the reception at the council offices the day that announcement was the big headline in the local evening newspaper the *South Wales Echo*. Hammam was calling him everything under the sun and his remarks were very homophobic, then, when we got in front of Rodney Berman, Sam was totally charming and congratulated him. He was like two different blokes that day and he could be like that. He could be very engaging, very witty sometimes and those doe-ey eyes would look at you. Sometimes if he did not like something he would take you aside and ask what was going on. 'Don't you like me, I like you, why can't we be brothers and friends' – it was all a show and I saw through that very early.

Sam did do many good things for Cardiff City Football Club, you can never take that away from him, but it all came at an enormous cost that haunted the club for more than a decade. He took over Cardiff City from chairman Steve Borley at the end of 2000 on the basis he would provide new investment. Hammam was handed the keys to a club that had very little debt but was playing in the lowest level of the Football League – then the Third Division – in front of small crowds of a few thousand at a decaying Ninian Park ground. The best thing that could be said about the stadium was that it was traditional.

Steve Borley had started the process of moving to a new stadium. He was arguably the visionary, along with council leader Russell Goodway, in getting Cardiff council to agree in principle to the idea of a move from their historic home to the other side of Ninian Park Road, where there was a council-owned athletics stadium and a decent area of development land. Shortly after that agreement Hammam took control of Cardiff City with 82.5% of the club's shares being held by Rudgwick, a London-based company which had brothers Sam and Ned Hammam as the two directors. According to their financial statements of 31 May 2005, Sam Hammam owned all the shares and controlled Rudgwick which then ran Cardiff City as their subsidiary. It turned out the football club's finances were included as part of Rudgwick's accounts.

Sam spent huge money on players, got Cardiff promoted twice and firmed up the original stadium plans put in place by Steve Borley. He had a vision, a dream, and was very good at selling that idea to people, particularly the press and fans. He spent large sums at Cardiff City. Many of us believe much of it was spent unwisely, and if that had been his own money then it would simply have been up to him. However the vast majority of the money spent was not his gift to the club – it was borrowed by the club on his say-so, which became a key distinction. He also took plenty of money out in management fees. It has taken a lot to stave off the problems created by Sam Hammam in those early years. It is only the arrival of Malaysian owner Vincent Tan that has allowed Cardiff City to move on. All football clubs have debts, but it is the way they are structured, arranged and paid for that matters – whether they are under control or not. Cardiff's were not.

Despite that he has to take some of the credit for signing the Conditional Development Agreement with Cardiff council in 2004. That was the basis to everything that has happened since, and ultimately took Cardiff City to the Premier League. He understood that unless we did something with the stadium in Cardiff then the football club was not going to survive. Council leader Russell Goodway was doing it for the good of the city, while Sam wanted success for the football club. We also need to pay tribute to the late club chief executive David Temme who was doing the hard yards behind the scenes. However it all had to go through lots of reincarnations before it would work out finally.

According to the Cardiff City Business Plan, June 2003, Revision A, the aim was for a new stadium which would be open for the 2005/6 season, with 30,000 seats and the potential to expand to 60,000. At one stage the plan was even more ambitious, 45,000 seats with the ability to expand further. Sam was right about one thing – the new stadium was needed to fund a team to compete in Division One and reach the Premier League. The economic case in favour included the fact there were 1.8 million people within less than an hour of the ground and no other top football club in the area at the time, backing up the idea that Cardiff was a potential sleeping giant. Hammam had the aim of representing Wales, much to the annoyance of Swansea City fans an hour down the road, and thought he had spotted an opportunity.

The Business Plan was optimistic in a lot of ways. It said they were aiming for promotion to the Premiership by 2008/9, within three seasons of the new stadium being open. There was a proposed loan account to fund the playing staff with £15m earmarked to maintain Division One status and attain a place in the Premiership. The total project cost, including retail and a 154-bed hotel, was put at £95–100 million. The Business Plan put forward by Hammam and the club in 2004 argued:

> Whilst the cash flows initially show high levels of speculative capital expenditure there is sufficient evidence to demonstrate that the returns from football can sustain and repay all loans within normal commercial terms.
>
> In addition and significantly, the business is owned and managed by Sam Hammam who has the expertise and experience at the highest levels of football to achieve the plan – providing the new stadium is made available to the club to enable it to capture the revenues required.

Cardiff council was expected to give away the value of the retail park land at Leckwith and Ninian Park, estimated at £40.6 million in the business plan, as their contribution to the development. Also the club and council would both contribute the proceeds from the sale of the land which held the old football ground at Ninian Park, where the club had a 99-year lease on council-owned land. That was estimated to be another £7.48 million between them. All those figures changed over the years, but even then there was a considerable shortfall which was to be covered by retail revenues and by investment from Cardiff City Football Club. There were quite a few holes in this business strategy and it did not get off the ground. Obviously other people did not trust so completely in Hammam's 'expertise and experience at the highest levels of football to achieve the plan.'

In particular, Cardiff council laid down eight conditions which were never close to being fully satisfied under Hammam. They included the demand that Cardiff City Football Club's financial arrangements were to be provided on an 'open book basis', the council must be satisfied the club could raise sufficient funds and revenues to ensure the council would provide no additional funding. Those conditions showed the council needed to be fully confident that the club could survive and deliver, because Cardiff City going into insolvency or into administration was a very real threat on an almost daily basis during that period. Being covered for that situation was a huge part of all the negotiations and planning for the council.

The rest of the conditions were about such things as providing a Park and Ride bus facility from the ground on non-match days, all much more straightforward. The council were determined to see something that would benefit the city of Cardiff, not line the pockets of one person or a handful of people. They would not proceed unless the major points of the eight conditions were met in full.

By this stage I was a co-director with Paul Guy at PMG, a property development company based in Cardiff. We had persuaded Capital and Regional PLC to look into the Cardiff City project, despite Hammam's absurd behaviour with their retail chief executive Andrew Lewis-Pratt. We were going back and fore to London for endless meetings to thrash out the proposals to deliver the project and in the end we became consultants for them to help put the retail park together. This was a time when the football club was in dire financial straits, so C&R were lending money to support the club so we would have time to get the property deal done. Paul and I gave money in a loose sponsorship arrangement which saw £3 million go to the club from ourselves and C&R because the football club still had overall responsibility for both parts of the project, the stadium and the retail. By the way – the club accounts showed £500,000 management fees were going into Rudgwick, in fact there were management fees every year, so our money was helping to make that possible as well!

That £3 million kept the football club and the retail development project going while we tried to put the deal together, without it everything would have fallen apart immediately. Because of the complexity of the deal we had to move very quickly into a more involved role in the football club as well as the stadium development. From starting in a consultancy position with C&R, PMG moved to a 50/50 arrangement with them to jointly fund and develop the retail park – eventually we would buy them out and have full responsibility for everything. In the end, because Cardiff City were never in a position to repay us, we effectively wrote off the £3 million debt with some sponsorship for the club.

During this period we met Sam several times at the football club and went up to London to meet him on a few other occasions. He wanted to have it all, all of the time. What he did at Wimbledon was at the back of everybody's mind, particularly the Cardiff council officials. Wimbledon AFC fans still talk about the betrayal to this day after they were left without a ground or a football club, while Hammam was left with an estimated £36 million. He sold their Plough Lane ground to Safeway for £8 million and sold the club to a Norwegian group who hoped to move it to Dublin. Wimbledon eventually moved to Milton Keynes and became the MK Dons under different owners. You cannot go into a project like the proposed Cardiff City Stadium, which is a genuine public/private partnership, with the possibility of someone trying to make their own gains out of it. The council were trying to do something good for the city, the future of the football club and could not take that risk.

Almost everyone had some concerns about dealing with Hammam. Peter Ridsdale succeeded Sam as chairman and he summed it up in his submission to the High Court in 2008:

> In my experience Sam is difficult to work with. I encountered three key difficulties: the lack of corporate governance at the club, Sam's attitude that it was 'his club', and his volatile management style.
>
> Sam's volatile style was also difficult to manage. He bullied employees and would often 'blow up' and shout and swear in meetings, even in front of advisors, banks and people he was doing business with. His behaviour sometimes embarrassed me and the

Club. I acted as a buffer between Sam and employees, professional advisors and the companies and institutions we dealt with (especially the council).

Sam told HMRC [Her Majesty's Revenue and Customs] he was not paying the tax bill because he wanted to buy players and would pay them what was owed 'eventually'. The professionals were told they would be paid back when the stadium was built.

The professional advisors and David Temme had a meeting with Sam at one point to tell him he needed a more buildable project. They raised the fact that Sam was paying himself £500,000 a year [in management fees]. David told me Sam's response was 'that it was none of their business'.

Once I was deputy chairman I stopped Sam having a company chequebook.

That sums up pretty well what he was like.

Towards the end of Hammam's time at Cardiff City I was summoned to have afternoon tea with him in the up-market Claridges Hotel in the centre of London. It was very strange occasion, he was just objectionable. You sat there having afternoon tea with him in these plush surroundings. On the face of it he was entirely personable and chatty and friendly, but you never got anywhere with him and you constantly felt like you were wasting your time. If you were not telling him something he liked then he was not interested, it was as simple as that. He was saying it had to be done his way or no way, I came out of there thinking the whole thing was not going to work at all. He was not going to listen to the business plan advice and was not going to listen to other points either, it is really frustrating when somebody is that awkward. If you said one thing, he would just say the opposite all day for the sake of it. You could not get through to him. He believes what he thinks is always right, he truly believes it, and that makes him the most difficult man to deal with I have ever known.

I think he had a bomb-proof feeling – and why not? He achieved much success with Wimbledon – reaching the First Division, winning the FA Cup and walking away with a lot of money – and then got Cardiff City two promotions as well. He had the club's supporters onside, he gave a lot of access to the more vociferous fans to keep them onside – he was very clever in his marketing of himself.

It was just that he borrowed too much money, spent too much money and got himself into a huge hole. The council were always aware they were giving away a very large amount of valuable land to go into the stadium project. This also had to be sanctioned by the Welsh Assembly Government, because it was effectively a grant to the football club. You can see the benefits for Cardiff and Wales coming out of it now, but there were plenty of pitfalls they had to avoid.

One person who played a crucial role in keeping the project alive from 2003 until 2005 was David Temme, then the Cardiff City chief executive. Sadly he died in 2011, but his role in the success of the stadium has been greatly underplayed. He understood the project. He was an engineer by background and he led in the early days, with Sam one step removed from the interface with the council and others. There was a huge amount of work already done before we became involved again in 2005 – road designs, impact studies on the retail, the ramifications of another major development, transport and environment reports – and crucially they had also got planning consent.

Paul Guy was a central figure in all of this. He remembers:

I was involved with David Temme at Cardiff Devils ice hockey team and we had an idea that you could pool the management, ticketing and so on between the ice hockey, football and rugby in Cardiff, while keeping the clubs absolutely separate. It was something that works well in the US, so we decided to get involved at Cardiff City as well in 1999.

At the time Sam Kumar was Cardiff City chairman; we put money in and converted it into shares. Steve Borley, Kim Walker and Michael Isaacs came in and also put up some money, I think we started to push the club forward but maybe we had taken it as far as we could. Then Sam Hammam really came out of the blue.

I wasn't unhappy to see him come in, I just wanted to see the club do as well as possible and he seemed as though he was a knight in shining armour. However it soon became apparent he was a complete maverick and regarded it as 'his club.'

Everyone saw through what he was – he got away with it at Wimbledon but he was not going to get away with it a second time down here in Wales. The money that was wasted in a couple of seasons was not very clever.

I have dealt with some odd people in property so I was not afraid to stand up to him, but eventually that was why I wanted to get out towards the end of 2004. It got to the stage where there was no point in me staying as a director. You could not fulfil the normal duties of a director because we were not given enough financial information, we did not know what was happening, so it was a pretty uncomfortable position to be in.

Paul resigned towards the end of 2004, while fellow board members Kim Walker and Michael Isaacs stepped down for similar reasons in April and June 2005, respectively. In Peter Ridsdale's 2008 High Court submission he reported:

Sam did not do business in a transparent way. Directors Steve Borley, Michael Isaacs and Kim Walker told me that Sam would not show them financial information and that there were very few, if any, board meetings. Sam actually told me not to share financial information with the directors. I observed that David Temme would get in trouble with Sam if he shared financial information in this way. Later, when my new finance director Tony Brown circulated financial information to the board, Sam went wild. He did not like board directors to have copies of documents and did not want the directors to talk to each other or to senior executives of the club. Sam's decisions tended to be presented as fait accompli so that any discussion was after the fact. Sam would often cover the lack of hard information with vague phrases about honour, hearts and minds, and so on.

David [Temme] notes his instructions from Sam that John Rozier [the previous finance director] must not give them [the Directors] any information.' This was even when they were being asked to invest further in the club. According to David's note, Sam said they would invest 'with an open heart and an open mind,' and, when David Temme expressed his concern at the instructions, Sam cut the meeting short.

Peter added that behaviour from Hammam sounded familiar to him; it did to all of us. After taking the controlling stake in Cardiff City, Hammam oversaw promotion from the old Third Division in 2001 and then again in 2003 to Division One, now called the Championship, under experienced manager Lennie Lawrence. That came in a thrilling final at the Millennium Stadium in Cardiff, while Wembley was being redeveloped. They were playing QPR, the game went into extra-time and Wales's striker Robert Earnshaw was taken off for Andy Campbell, who had been bought for £1 million from Middlesbrough but struggled to nail down a starting place. Campbell scored with a long range lob to spark massive celebrations in Cardiff. Hammam also spent £1 million buying Ireland international Graham Kavanagh and £1.7 million on striker Peter Thorne. The wage bill of £8.3m exceeded earnings comfortably and the 'high levels of speculative capital expenditure', as the business plan put it, went flying up despite promotion. Growing debt was a simpler way of putting it.

One fee that was in the accounts, despite the huge debts, was up to £600,000 a year to Hammam's company, Rudgwick, for 'management services'. Peter Ridsdale explained in his 2008 High Court submission:

> The club is 100 % owned by Cardiff City Holdings. During Sam's period as owner, 82.5% of the shares in the Holdings were owned by Rudgwick Ltd, a company owned and controlled by Sam. Rudgwick's initial investment shares in Holdings were shown on the balance sheet [of Cardiff City] as a debt to Rudgwick. Rudgwick even charged the club interest. I put a stop to that and had the debt written off. I had no discussion with Sam about Rudgwick other than at a later date to stop the management fees the club was paying to it. Sam's salary had always been paid to Rudgwick as management fees. I had found that Rudgwick was

accruing in its accounts for £1.5 million unpaid management fees. I refused to allow this as the club could not afford it. As part of his severance deal we agreed to pay £200,000 as a lump sum plus £100,000 a year for three years.

By May 2004 Cardiff City's debts had risen to £31 million with £21.8 million owed to Citibank, who were pressing hard for their money back. Peter Ridsdale told the High Court in 2008:

> Sam told me he had restructured the Citibank debt using loan notes. I later discovered that Sam arranged the Citibank loan through his contact there, Nicholas Saloum [*sic*.]. Citibank then asked for the loan to be repaid. I understand there was a very uncomfortable meeting where Sam lost his temper with Nicholas Saloum for getting him into this situation and the other Citibank people said absolutely nothing and did not come to Saloum's support. In any event, the Citibank loan needed to be repaid.

'Nicollas Salloum' was the correct spelling, someone who started his career in Bahrein before moving to Paris and then London. He is now chief executive of a capital management company for wealthy families, based in Switzerland, a role he started in July 2004 after leaving Citibank.

Payments of £22m on 30 September 2004, and £2m on 15 October 2004, were transferred to Cardiff City, from a mysterious group called Langston. To add to the mystery it was an unsecured loan arranged by Hammam, that was then due to be paid back in 2011. Citibank were paid off thanks to the Langston loan in September 2004. Something had obviously been needed, but taking the loan from Langston was an action that would come to hang over the club like the sword of Damocles for years to come.

Who are Langston? That is a question that has been asked countless times. We all have theories we are pretty confident about, but we have never been able to get official confirmation. We did try, very hard. Langston was registered in Panama on 8 September 2004, and the only two shares are not owned by people, as would be more common, but by two companies registered in the British Virgin Islands, an offshore financial haven with complete secrecy. That trail ends there, with no record of either of those companies being involved in any other British business. When we approached Pictet and Cie, a private bank based in Switzerland that was channelling the money from Langston, they would only confirm they had 'carried out strict due diligence in relation to the Langston Group, its past and present financial holdings and its beneficial ownership and were at all times satisfied with the results of our inquiries.' That was that, then, but those sketchy details would prove enough to satisfy Cardiff council's understandable concerns about money-laundering – just – once Cardiff City Football Club were moved one step away from the new stadium development. As for our theory, well, if Langston is not substantially controlled by Hammam himself, then who else would have given £24 million to Cardiff City on an unsecured basis?

Despite the Langston loan, which effectively just changed the name of who was owed the money, there were still considerable debts of around £30 million. Wales internationals Robert Earnshaw, Danny Gabbidon and James Collins were sold, striker Earnshaw to West Bromwich Albion for £3 million in 2004, while defenders Collins and Gabbidon went to West Ham in a £3.5 million transfer in 2005. They also sold Kavanagh to Wigan that season for around £400,000 to help cut the wage bill and pay some more of the debts. Former Southampton manager Dave Jones took charge on the field in 2005 and was able to keep the team mid-table in the Championship even though he had to sell such top players.

Despite raising around £7 million over 12 months through those transfers, there was also a £1.6 million bill to be paid to the Inland Revenue, rising with interest as it was put off. All in all it was last chance saloon and Hammam's 'expertise' did not seem to be working. Hammam recruited former Leeds chairman Peter Ridsdale as a consultant in 2005. In his 2008 High Court submission, Ridsdale revealed:

> Financially when I arrived the club was living from hand to mouth. Payment of both major trade creditors and long term borrowing was supposed to come from the proposed new stadium development and the expectations on this front were unrealistic.
>
> By the time I joined the club, the [Stadium] Project was stalled. C&R [our partners Capital and Regional] would not even take my calls – they thought the project was dead and were not interested. In the club's accounts, unconditionality was booked as September 2005, but even this was completely unrealistic. Sam was impatient and could not accept there were a series of steps to be gone through. He always wanted unconditionality tomorrow.

'Unconditionality' effectively meant the official go-ahead for the project, it would have satisfied all the conditions. For Hammam to be able to pull a rabbit out of the hat, he needed the rapid go-ahead for the new stadium with the money that would release from the retail side. However it was never going to work under Sam Hammam, he simply did not have the business approach, local knowledge and reputation to get this particular deal through in Wales. Cardiff council were understandably cautious and they commissioned Deloittes accountants to undertake a detailed report on Sam's plans. They reported back on 6 June 2005. The Executive Summary revealed:

> The club has pursued a policy of 'planned losses' over the last three years which has resulted in a net debt as of 31 May 2004, of £29.1m. That is estimated to be the fourth highest debt in the Championship; the average is £14m.
>
> The club restructured its debt in September 2004, with the issue of 24m of fixed rate unsecured redeemable loan stock until 2011. Debt is estimated to have increased to 31.8m.
>
> In our view it is highly unlikely that the club will be able to break-even at this level in Ninian Park. A more prudent

assumption is that the club will continue to lose £3–4m per season at an operating level (before interest).

Interest of £1.5m 2003/4, a charge of £2m 2004/5, is likely to be deferred. That is a relatively high charge for a Championship club and places the club at a competitive disadvantage.

We estimate the club would have debts of over £50m if it enters the new stadium in time for the 2006/7 season. Debts would increase further if entry was delayed to the 2007/8 season.

We consider it highly unlikely that the club would be able to reduce the debt level while playing in the new stadium in the Championship in the foreseeable future.

After 2008 the interest and other charges on the outstanding loan stock become so significantly greater with the returns attached more akin to mezzanine finance.

There is limited scope for the club to refinance the current debt in the foreseeable future – even if Premiership status was secured. The debt level could only be reduced by a debt for equity swap by the loan stock holders or by utilising any revenue increases from the Premiership promotion as a pure 'windfall' to help clear debts with no investment in strengthening the playing squad or wage increases.

The club will therefore be dependent, to a large extent, on the continued support of the major investing shareholders – primarily we understand this to be Sam Hammam.

Overview of business plan

Updates to the club's business plan have been received in February 2005 and July 2004 although the plan has not been updated significantly for two years. It remains extremely high level in many areas – particularly in regard to support for the club's trading projections in the new stadium.

In our view the current football environment is such that it will be extremely difficult for the club to gain promotion to the Premiership even in the new stadium.

Comments on business plan revenues.

The facilities at Ninian Park are extremely limited and compare unfavourably with the majority of Championship grounds. We recognise the club can expect to benefit significantly from a move to a new stadium.

The club's implied projection of spend per attendee in the new stadium appears challenging in comparison to other championship clubs.

The club has not done the necessary market research to properly understand its fanbase and potential ticket sales.

The club's assumption of total attendance of 21,600 appears challenging. We consider a figure of 19,600 to be more achievable. Overall we consider forecast ticketing revenues for the first year in the new stadium to be potentially overstated by up to 9%.

No research or evidence has been made available to us to support the club's projections for corporate hospitality. We consider revenue from this area of £2.5m per annum to be highly ambitious. An income of £1.25m may be a more realistic projection.

The club has projected £1m per annum for five years for the stadium/stand naming rights revenues. We consider this assumption to be extremely challenging and, based on recent comparable UK naming rights deals, consider annual revenue of £150–300k to be more realistic.

The club assumed £3m debenture rights, but in the Championship these would be 'immaterial'.

We predict an 18% decrease from business plan which, without cuts in playing budget, would mean losses of £6.4m from football activities in 2006/7.

To break even in the new stadium in the Championship we estimate the club would need to reduce squad spending to £7.1m before interest and £4.9m to break even after interest charges. This level of spending should be sufficient to maintain Championship status. However Premiership status would be very unlikely to be achieved on such a budget and relegation to League One would be a realistic risk.

We have not reviewed overheads but note that the budgeted costs are lower than recorded in 2003/4 by £0.7m (including a £0.6m management charge from the ultimate parent company (Rudgwick) – we have not seen any supporting evidence to determine whether these charges are based on arms length commercial arrangements). The club's business plan includes no provision for such management charges.

In our view it would be challenging to secure significant external financing.

As for the threat of administration, 40 football clubs have gone into administration, no Premiership club but numerous ambitious clubs who could not maintain Premier League status have suffered this fate.

It is likely Cardiff City football club would withstand administration but creditors would lose substantially.

Conclusion
The council may include wider benefits for the city…
However, given the uncertainty surrounding the club's financial position, we recommend that the council should ensure that it is adequately protected in all its contractual dealings with the club. All contracts should include provisions to deal with the situation were the club to enter into insolvency proceedings before completion of the new stadium or during its occupancy of the new stadium.

It was a damning indictment on almost every level, made more so by the understated language. To sum up, Hammam and the football club's estimates of revenue were extremely 'challenging', while the mounting debts meant there was little prospect of sustaining a challenge for the Premiership and relegation from the Championship was more likely. The club going bust was also highly possible because of the scale and likely increase of the debt. Debts of more than £50 million would be unsustainable for anyone outside the Premiership – and hard to cope with even there.

No council could have ignored that report and there was no way they could give Hammam what he wanted on the back of the evidence available. That meant Hammam's plans had nowhere to go. There is no doubt the club was facing administration and the stadium plan was facing collapse, along with the retail park, at this stage in 2005. That was when PMG were involved again.

On 18 November 2005, chief executive Byron Davies wrote in a report to Cardiff council:

> The uncertainty of information relating to construction costs
> and associated fees remains, together with the unresolved issues
> attached to the disposal of retail land and the absence of firm
> information about external sources of finance [the Langston loan]
> As such it is not possible to say the project is viable. The financial
> viability of the project has not been proved.

What had become apparent was that Sam, as owner, chairman and majority shareholder of Cardiff City, was being left to his own devices on the football club side, which included their contribution to the stadium. He had several consultants in there racking up huge fees and he was not paying them anything, all that work was being done on account. He said he was trying to build another Nou Camp, like Barcelona's stadium which at just under 100,000 seats is the largest in Europe. That was far too ambitious for the available funding or support levels. The council saw through this and there was no credibility in the numbers, his figures, his projections or his design. That was a real crunch time and we had to take control of that side of it for the whole thing to go ahead. Our first involvement was through the retail park, but that was going to fall by the wayside if the stadium did not happen, every part needed to work out if the club was to survive.

I don't know if Sam did the right things football-wise before we got there, but by 2006 he had absolutely no chance in terms of the stadium development and keeping that club going. The sensible people at Cardiff council, like project manager Emyr Evans and chief executive Byron Davies, could see straight through him. The politicians were worried, they didn't want to be seen doing something with this man which could come back to haunt them, so they were behind the officers of the council. Ironically Sam was so pleased with the support from the Labour party group who controlled the council that he urged Cardiff City supporters to vote for them. His support didn't do them much good, they lost the

2004 election and were replaced by a Liberal-Democrat-led coalition along with the Conservatives.

The project was making some progress going into 2006. Deloittes provided another report to the council on 27 April 2006. It recognised the change for the better of the management with then vice-chairman Peter Ridsdale and finance director Tony Brown coming in, plus more professional advisors, which included PMG. It commented on the revised business plan, which a few of us were involved in producing. In particular Tony Brown and Richard Gee, from KSS Richards, who did all the back-breaking work to produce hundreds of pages of detail. They were the architects of putting together a very professional business plan that ultimately was accepted by the council. It was a more substantial document in every sense – it was about five times the size of the old business plan even before you looked at the improved level of content. However even that impressive bit of work could not paper over all the cracks. The football club's net debt on the 28 February 2006, despite all the player sales, was £27.1 million, plus an overdue £700,000 owed to the Inland Revenue and a standstill agreement with professional advisors who were owed £1.6 million in relation to the new stadium at that stage – all that was just from the evidence available to Deloittes.

Average attendances at Ninian Park had dropped to around 11,750, the club put that down to unease among fans about the financial position. Under Dave Jones the club had improved slightly on the field to finish in the top half of the Championship, only just, compared to the previous two seasons when they finished in the bottom half of the table but crucially did enough to avoid relegation.

The Deloittes report added: 'Without a successful renegotiation of [the Langston] loan stock the club could have debts of £35m upon entering the new stadium in 2008/9. The debt would grow rapidly as after 2008 the interest and other charges on the outstanding loan stock become significantly greater.'

It was clear the council were not satisfied at a Business Plan meeting on 13 July 2006. Council head of legal Geoff Shimmell made the point that he did not believe they had enough information on the Langston loan notes terms for council investment. They also required accurate up-to-date accounts and details of any required shortfall funding. Cardiff City had not provided the open-book accounting that was one of the required eight conditions. The delay on providing information on the loan note holders, in other words revealing who was behind Langston, was clearly causing a potentially terminal delay – everyone was concerned about where the money had really come from and worried about possible repercussions.

Sam's approach to the football club was causing problems as well, not helped by the way he boasted to the press, talking about possible new signings which appealed to the fans. On 16 August Paul Guy sent an e-mail to Richard Gee:

> We are reviewing our position given Sam's total disregard to the wages cap in the business plan. To read the *Echo* tonight and read Sam quoting he will still be buying one, two or three more players is totally reckless behaviour. We now have serious doubts over the whole viability of this development progressing. We are not providing another penny to the club until this deal goes unconditional which we cannot now see happening as the business plan and the cash flow are unsustainable. Unless Sam or Ned come up with the funds, the club will not be able to pay the September wages and all bets are off.

Paul drafted a letter to Sam three days later:

> As you are aware Mike Hall and I met Peter Ridsdale and Tony Brown to discuss the very serious deterioration of the club's financial position in respect of the business plan submitted to the council. Despite your personal assurance and your repeated comments to the press that players wages would be kept within the business plan, the current position is an overspend of about £1.5m. The cash flow projections we were given show a shortfall

of £709,000 at the end of September. There is also an assumption that C&R will be contributing a further £1m in October and that you will receive a further £1.5m in December in the form of a contribution towards costs [which was all jointly funded by C&R and PMG].

We have made our position absolutely clear on a number of occasions that the final £1m from C&R is only forthcoming when the project goes unconditional. This has always been assumed to be 6 December. If the club's cash flow projections are adjusted to reflect this the month end cash shortage is £709,000 in September, £927,000 in October, £1,647,000 in November. This position is clearly unsustainable.

Given this position I cannot see how the club can convince the council in respect of the Business Plan viability. There is no prospect if getting planning in September. Unless you introduce additional cash resources into the club this whole project will fail. This is extremely disappointing given that all the property issues are largely resolved and we would have been ready to start by December 2006.

In conclusion unless you can provide solid evidence of new funds being introduced into the club we intend to stand down the whole professional team within 14 days of this letter. We will of course have to notify the council of our decision and the reasons why.

At this stage Langston accepted the principle of swapping the proceeds of naming rights for the new stadium in return for reducing the debt, but not down to the £9 million amount we had suggested in line with council guidance, along with making the loan interest free for a period and restructuring the overall debt to delay the final payment.

The writing was still on the wall in the second half of 2006, the situation at Cardiff City was desperate, as illustrated by an internal memorandum on 2 October from finance director Tony Brown to Sam, Peter, Ned Hammam, Steve Borley and Jonathan Crystal QC (a Cardiff City director at the time). It had some dark tidings.

The club was only able to honour the payroll last Thursday

28 September 2006, by withholding the following payments due to the Inland Revenue as instructed:

> July PAYE £306.000. August PAYE £330,000. Payment of old PAYE arrears £157,000.
>
> - The club has received notification from the Inland Revenue today querying why they have not received payments for two months and demanding immediate re-payment.
> - There are obvious concerns of the potential impact of any negative publicity of our cash position especially given the current success on the pitch.
> - The club is now not in a position to continue to make normal trading payments and we are fielding a barrage of Trade Creditor calls.
>
> Please can you advise how the club should respond to the Inland Revenue and deal with the immediate cash position.

If you do not pay the players then you are in breach of contract and risk making them free agents, meaning you lose out on potential transfer fees. That could have cost the club many millions, which is why they were taking the extraordinary step of putting off paying tax instead. The following day PMG lawyer Eamonn Cannon wrote to Cardiff City's legal advisor Alan Whiteley saying: 'It would appear to me to be the case that either fresh capital is found urgently or the directors must resolve to wind up the company and take steps to appoint a provisional liquidator.' That view was fleshed out by Paul Guy in an email to Peter Ridsdale on 5 October 2006:

> We are faced with a current position that the October wages will not be met, about £1m is owed to the Inland Revenue, and by February 2007 a cash deficit of £2m+ will be due to the project delay. We [Capital Retail Partnership] will not put any further cash into the club until Sam can demonstrate that at least £4m of cash is injected into the club to get it into a stable financial position...
>
> I am sorry to be so negative but the end of the road has been reached as far as we are concerned. In our opinion without the cash injection there is no future for this scheme.

The vital process of sorting out Langston and importance of getting a proper business plan in place did not get through to Sam. His argument was that they should just give him the money, start the project and let him get on with it. It is maybe a little strange to look back now, but the situation really was that bleak.

The response from the club two weeks later was a plan that involved Seymour Pierce investment bank offering shares to raise £3 million, but that did not generate much interest so insolvency still seemed the most likely option for Cardiff City.

Apart from the problems around the huge and mysterious Langston debt, the Inland Revenue and the professional consultants had served notice on the club which meant it would be closed down unless several million pounds could be found. PMG had been willing to put up £9 million to ensure the future of the stadium and retail project, but that too was threatened because of the uncertainty. What was the point of putting all that money in to save the retail park if the project was still going to collapse because of the way the football club was being run?

Quite simply, unless something changed dramatically, the club was going to run out of funds and go bust at the start of 2007. That would have meant an automatic points reduction, almost certain relegation and staying at the old Ninian Park for the foreseeable future. Cardiff City was staring at financial ruin and a generation in the lower levels of the Football League. Hammam owned 82.5% of Cardiff City and he would not recognise that reality, blocking the only actions that could stop it happening. We had to find a way of changing that.

Paul and I had one final meeting with Sam to try to get him to see sense, but it was useless. The decision was made that, by hook or by crook, he simply had to go.

2

The Back of Sam – or so we thought!

THE WHISPERS AROUND the council corridors were that they would simply not do a deal with this man, Sam Hammam. That was not our fault, but that was the way it was. Peter Ridsdale explained in his 2008 High Court submission:

> The council always had certain concerns about 'Who they were doing business with'. Sam Hammam personally was not considered in a positive light by the council. The council told me not to bring Sam to meetings or it was all off. Sam attended once, in autumn 2006. One of the items appearing in the Business Plan was mentioned [the club's board, including Sam, had agreed the Business Plan unanimously]. Sam said: 'I won't consider that.' It was pointed out this was already in the Business Plan. Sam said he hadn't read the Business Plan and that we had no intention of implementing it – it had only been put in to keep the council happy. I had to explain that Sam had not meant what he said. The council told me to take him out.

The only way to get the stadium and retail park through was to set up a separate development company at arm's length from Cardiff City Football Club, Devco as it was known, which was to become Cardiff City Stadium Ltd (CCS). That new company would also deal with the various professional companies who had been working on the project.

On 7 April 2006, Paul Guy wrote to Peter Ridsdale: 'The situation is obviously complicated by the historical debt owed to the professional team and their reluctance, with which we totally concur, to undertake any further work for the club without first having certainty of payment and satisfaction of previous debt. So the solution is to set up a DEVCO to take full responsibility. The council is in favour of this approach.'

Senior and influential politicians such as Welsh Assembly Government First Minister Rhodri Morgan and former Labour Party leader Neil Kinnock – both big sports fans and in particular Cardiff City fans – were also keen on a Devco as it would remove some of their concerns. Paul was asking Peter to consult with Sam and the board about this idea of how to move forward with the redevelopment.

CCS would receive the revenue from the council and the football club from the sale of Ninian Park, as well as the retail proceeds through Capital Retail Park Partnership (at that stage PMG along with Capital and Regional). This Devco would then build the new football stadium, whilst the retail park partnership (us and C&R) would build everything else – the retail park, the replacement athletics stadium, the planned House of Sport and the improved road system. The people on the board of the Devco would be Paul Guy, Peter Ridsdale and myself – we could not have Sam on it, so initially Ned Hammam represented the Cardiff City owner but he did not last long.

There was still a long way to go, but that was an essential first step. It included PMG agreeing shortfall funding of £7 million, a figure that quickly rose to £9 million as the costs of the project grew. Eventually the figure was more than £11 million, which included an extra £2.3 million guarantee to cover any building overrun on the stadium. Again this decision was driven by the debt which was threatening the football club and therefore the stadium project.

On top of all the other debts, by now more than £2 million was owed to consultants for work they had done on the football and athletics stadia. They were Holder Mathias architects, Ove Arup and partners engineers and builders, project managers Davis Langdon, and Savill, Bird and Axon, independent transport consultants. Their total fees for the work they had done in good faith was £2,141,406.90, in theory to be paid when the contract with the council went unconditional. The problem was that as long as Sam was involved, the project was not going to go unconditional. Before the end of 2006, PMG paid almost £100,000 of fees on behalf of the club simply to keep the project moving forward. Also we had decided Sam had to go.

Paul and I had a meeting with him trying to agree his exit from the club, the repayment to Langston, control of the football stadium, the council, the business plan – all those issues which needed sorting. We sat with him for more than six exhausting hours in the offices of Nabarro's, our lawyers in London, when we were trying to thrash out a deal with him. He had his financial advisor there and his lawyer. Eventually he agreed heads of terms and he signed them. Then he stormed off into the reception. I went and sat with him there and told him it was a sensible deal he had done, but he felt he had been forced to give everything away. He walked out of the offices onto the London streets still upset, but I thought that after an extremely long day we had a deal.

The next morning he woke up and said he was not doing it. That is the type of individual you were dealing with. He always thought there was a better deal – even though he had signed an agreement in principle. Unfortunately the agreement he had signed was not legally binding.

It came to the crunch with Sam, with a make-or-break deadline looming. Time was running out on the Development Agreement with the council, due to lapse on 31 December 2006. As it turned out we were able to extend this into 2007 to complete the deal, it took a lot of persuasion to earn this sort of extension and it only happened because the council could see progress had been made.

Sam had brought former Leeds United chairman Peter Ridsdale in to assist. Peter soon understood what needed to be done and switched sides, if you like. It meant that we, along with Peter, had to manoeuvre Sam out. The proposal was to reduce Hammam's shares from 82.5% of the club to 4%. He would also resign as chairman, all in return for new investment we had secured which would hopefully save the club.

However because of his controlling interest and involvement with Langston, we had to do it through negotiation. The scale of the Langston debt was too high for the stadium project figures to work if it was included in full in the Cardiff City accounts. We had to negotiate a reduction or Cardiff council were not going to go ahead. The council would have liked that debt to have come down to £10 million, but £15 million was arrived at as a figure which might be acceptable to both the council and Langston.

Of course Sam never admitted to being behind Langston, he claimed he was just their representative. The only other person who had any dealings with the club on behalf of Langston was a Swiss accountant called Philippe Tischauser, but he clearly had no authority on behalf of Langston and just reported back to an unknown person or persons. Strangely Hammam made sure he was not around on the first occasion Philippe Tischhauser came to Cardiff, as Peter Ridsdale told the High Court in 2008.

At a Cardiff City Stadium board meeting on 31 August 2006, attended by Paul Guy, Ned Hammam, Peter Ridsdale and myself, the loan notes were discussed with the aim of reducing the burden on the club to a level acceptable to the council. I pointed out that we had a deadline of 14 September to achieve this, in other words just two weeks later. Despite the urgency Ned said we must not take it for granted the loan note holders (Langston) would accept the proposals. For example the waiving of historical interest was not agreed. I stressed we were just trying to find a solution the council would accept.

People forget that the 'Langston issue' is really a 'Sam issue', not just in terms of who the money may have been owed to but more importantly because of why the money was owed to anyone at all. He spent that money on players, wages and bonuses – chasing the dream. He came into a club with virtually no debt in 2000, so that loan was given to cover money he spent since then. Peter Ridsdale pointed out in the 2008 High Court case:

> Sam always said 'I have put £30m into this club,' that was how he phrased it. I would counter saying this was debt and it was not the same. Sam would say 'It's as good as me' and 'this is my good name, I stand behind it.' I asked him if he was sure the Loan Notes were unsecured. He said yes, and that it would all be paid back from the project.
>
> Sam told me he could afford to take a £10 million hit on the Langston Loan Notes and it therefore seemed to me that he personally owned part of Langston. It may be that Sam's friends, family or associates, or a family trust, also benefit from Langston, and he may have someone else to answer to. However the material point is that Sam has acted towards the club as representing Langston in all substantive negotiations.

It was at that meeting, at the end of August 2006, PMG agreed in principle to increase the shortfall funding to £9 million, but with the security that the club could not buy or sell players or hire consultants without the agreement of Peter, who had to consult the Devco CCS or do it through independent funding. We also had first call on repayment from the club if they went into administration or insolvency, as a guarantee for the loan. That security was standard business practice for a loan of that scale, but it was to become a very important point.

At a meeting on 5 September 2006, it was agreed that Paul Guy and Peter Ridsdale would meet monthly to discuss club finances, formally agreeing there would be no player buying or selling, or hiring consultants, without agreement between them.

We also had to persuade the professional companies, who were owed large sums of money, to work with us. They agreed, on the understanding Sam would stay away from any decision-making.

The club was getting squeezed financially so we put together a group of investors who were prepared to put in a total of £6 million to keep it going – again all on the condition Sam went. Peter Ridsdale, Paul, Steve Borley and myself put in substantial amounts personally, but that £6 million was made up of contributions, large and small, from a lengthy list of Cardiff City fans. Effectively they were putting up their money to save the club. Those minority shareholders were also real heroes of this story, they know who they are and they played a huge part in getting Cardiff City to the Premier League. They deserve to get special enjoyment out of that achievement, knowing they all played a key role at a vital time.

After thinking we had agreed terms with Sam in London, only for him to back out, there was no alternative but to issue an irreversible ultimatum to him – get out or we will walk away, along with all those potential investors of £6m, and leave you to it. Cardiff City and Sam Hammam's D Day was 22 October 2006. Paul Guy takes up the story:

> This was the ultimate meeting. Without Sam going, no-one would put any money in. Without the money we would not have been able to continue trading and the administrators would have been called in.
>
> I went to Ninian Park with Mike and our lawyer Eamonn Cannon at 10am that morning. The two of them stayed downstairs and I went up to the boardroom where Sam was with club lawyer Alan Whiteley and Peter Ridsdale. It was a very quick conversation. It was, 'Sign these documents that will bring the investment in, you resign and your shares are diluted. You're out – or we will let you go into administration. You have until 12 o'clock.'
>
> There was no further conversation and I just left then, because he would only have started ranting and raving. I walked out of the boardroom and Sam then followed me downstairs. He saw Mike and Eamonn. Eamonn said, 'You picked the wrong day for a fight today, Sam.' I stayed and went back up to the boardroom, but Sam left the ground very shortly after that without having signed anything.
>
> I thought he would probably sign, that he had to, but we were never sure. If he had not then we had no choice about what we had to do. We had Price Waterhouse lined up to come in as

administrators straightaway, it was all in place. It was not a bluff by any stretch. You are not allowed to continue to trade when you are knowingly running up creditors, which is what Cardiff City would have been doing without the new investment.

Then at ten to twelve the papers were faxed through to Alan Whiteley at the club, signed by Sam and agreeing everything. Otherwise the club would have been gone, there is no question about that, Cardiff City was 10 minutes from disaster, but instead Sam was out at last.

It was a sense of relief because he was such an obstacle, the stadium was never going to happen with him there. Everyone had had a complete and utter gutsful of him by that time.

Yes, Sam did some good things for the club in the beginning, but when he took over there was next to no debt in there. He saddled this club with £30 million of debt. It really irks me now that as an unsecured creditor he has caused this club no end of grief. You can recognise that he did get that development agreement signed with the council, that is the plus side, but if you look at the negative side of what he left this club with then the thought of him ever coming back I think is simply wrong. I have no time for the man at all.

He was so lucky – there were a number of times when Mike and I look back and think we possibly should have taken the club into administration to wipe out that Langston debt and start again, but if we had then it would have delayed the new stadium plan. We would have missed the boat when the financial markets collapsed and it never would have happened, which is why he was still owed all that money.

It galls me when you hear him talk about never wanting to hurt the club, he has caused no end of problems.

With Sam gone, Peter Ridsdale came in as chairman and I joined the board of Cardiff City as a director along with Alan Whiteley. Paul and I became very involved in the design and costing of the football stadium because otherwise a crucial part of the jigsaw could not be delivered. We could start working sensibly with the council, who in turn were glad to be dealing with someone like Peter Ridsdale as chairman.

PMG was sucked into the football side of it all. We had

initially been happy to leave the football element to others, we were there for the property deal which was our area of expertise, but that was dependent on building a football stadium and an athletics stadium.

We went to the architects, along with the other consultants, and tried to do a deal with them, offering a fee structure which would keep them working but also give them a prospect of getting their money back eventually. Of course once the project went unconditional there was money in the pot to pay them, the problem was getting it there. If not then we had first security on our loan ahead of what was owed to them, so in reality they were unlikely to be paid and their best available choice was to work with us – and as a result they did all get paid in the end.

It was tortuous at the end of 2006. We were telling Hammam: 'Sam, you have to accept there are new investors coming on board, you have to accept the repayment structure and you are no longer chairman – you're out.' Unless you did the deal with Langston, the business plan would not add up and the council were not going to accept it, unless that happened then no cash would come in from the new investors to keep the football club going, without that it would not survive long enough for the project to go unconditional, without that then no-one was going be paid and the whole thing would collapse.

All these things came together on that one day when Sam signed away 78.5% of his control. £6 million came into the club and suddenly we could work sensibly with the council. Sam became more and more desperate over this period, he also thought there was a vendetta against him from all sorts of people, whether it was us, Peter or the council. He could not see what he had done wrong.

Even after Sam had reduced his involvement, there were still issues with the council looking to claw back income on crowds over 25,000. Peter Ridsdale's email response on 10 November 2006, was firm: 'I am stunned that after all the work that has gone into our new stadium project, keeping the club afloat, restructuring the debt, agreeing to rugby, and on the brink of getting the final go ahead, you now introduce changes to our agreement that stop this project in its tracks.'

Deloittes constructed another report for the council on 21 November 2006. This recognised that the club had improved the finances. We had sold striker Cameron Jerome to Birmingham in May 2006 for £2.9m. We had paid Inland Revenue arrears of £0.7m in September 2006. At that time Dave Jones had taken us to the top of the Championship, with an average attendance of 16,924. We had agreed the reduction of the loan stock debts to Langston to the more manageable £15 million, in return for the naming rights and with the added promise of a potential £5m bonus payment on promotion to the Premier League. However Deloittes pointed out that interest was now deferred rather than waived so 'we consider the agreement to be less favourable to the club than the one envisaged. The identity of the ultimate holders of the Loan Stock remains unknown, although the council has received a letter from the Loan Stock Holders' representative that the holders are individuals of good repute. The club has provided further details of its proposed transaction to introduce new investors into the club and reduce the role of Mr Sam Hammam in both the ownership and management of the club... we note the transaction remains work in progress.'

The report also recognised that the business plan was more thorough and prudent, the club were now committed to player sales if needed to balance books and they noted the positive developments since their phase one report.

That report cleared the way to extending the Development Agreement into 2007 to provide time to complete the deal. It was still touch and go. I had to ring council chief executive Byron Davies at home on New Year's Eve to get a three-month extension, with the council's legal expert Geoff Shimmell working on the details over that holiday period.

That was vital; in fact it turned out the whole project would have collapsed without it. If the original Development Agreement had lapsed, it would have been possible to draw up a new one but that would have taken time – probably several months. Given that the stadium project was up and running just before the economic crash of 2007/8, a delay of those 'several months' would have meant no chance of getting funding and the stadium going ahead.

Hammam was still pushing for certain conditions, which might be revealing about some of his motives. Club lawyer Alan Whiteley sent a letter to Geoff Shimmel at Cardiff council on 21 November 2006, saying they were looking to raise substantial funds through shares and stadium naming rights. Hammam also wanted a £5 million bonus if the club reached the Premier League and each year they retained that status. Hammam and Rudgwick would also be held 'harmless against any future claims by any party.'

Hammam wanted to have the honorary title of sole 'president' of the club for his life, six tickets for every home game and two for every away game, a parking space in the most prominent position and the right to visit every part of the ground, including the board room. The club would also agree to 'positively portray the time of Mr Sam Hammam's chairmanship of the club.'

Hammam's lawyer Peter Lloyd Cooper sent a discussion document which asked: 'If in the next five years any manager or executive wants to disclose information, Sam must first be notified and given an opportunity to respond.' If it wasn't so serious, those demands would be very funny. What was he so worried about? He was still a Cardiff City director and so he did get the title, the best parking space and continued to be a regular in the dressing room – but only until the end of December. Once everything was confirmed, the negotiations completed and Hammam was out of the club – we thought for good – Peter Ridsdale told the *South Wales Echo* at the start of January that the former club owner would only be welcome to come back if he bought a ticket – and presumably car parking!

The council were plainly relieved with their new partners.

Byron Davies wrote to council leader Rodney Berman on 26 November 2006: 'I must pay tribute to the council's staff and indeed CCFC and PMG for their endeavours to keep members informed through addressing in very tight timescales some of the most complex matters the council has had to deal with in my experience.'

On the agenda for Cardiff council Special Economic Scrutiny Committee, Atlantic Wharf, 1 December 2006, it said the new stadium was aimed at enhancing Cardiff as a European capital city. It outlined the background from the conditional agreement of 22 January 2004, between the council and football club along with Capital and Regional. Conditions included approval of the club's funding arrangements so the council could satisfy itself the project was viable. The club had to satisfy the council that income at the new stadium would service the debt, the council had to approve the club's development partners, while consent for the lease of the football stadium at a peppercorn rent was needed from the Welsh Assembly Government.

The council then had an executive business meeting on 7 December 2006, to recommend acceptance in principle of the club's business plan that we had all put together. They said the progress made by Cardiff City Football Club to satisfy the council's requirements since December 2005 had been good.

It said: 'The council's executive notes the considerable progress made on this project and the effective partnership arrangements in place between the council, CCS and PMG.' It recommended the council approve the business plan. It was a huge step forward, though far from the end of the road. Peter Ridsdale issued a press release which said:

> Today's announcement is truly a milestone for CCFC. From a position where the club's very existence was in question, we can now look forward to the day when we will be playing in a new stadium which will give us a real chance to compete with the very best in professional football.
>
> Apart from members of my own management team who have

worked day and night to help to get to today's announcement, I
must also thank Paul Guy and Mike Hall without whose help and
confidence this scheme would never have been possible... They
deserve the gratitude of every Cardiff City supporter.

When Cardiff City went up to the Premier League in 2013,
Hammam was a guest in the stand during the final home
game. There was talk in the papers about him becoming their
'Premiership Advisor.'

Now the Langston deal has been settled it is no longer
hanging over the club. I understand that Sam got a lot of his
money back from current Malaysian owner Tan Sri Dato Seri
Vincent. I am sure it is covered by confidentiality agreements –
and Sam got to sit there next to Tan in the sort of Life President
role he wanted. However most people have moved on, it is
Vincent Tan's club. He is the owner, he is running it and he is
certainly not dull. However it was strange seeing them arm in
arm after all the fighting and bad blood.

However if they let Hammam anywhere near that club
again in any meaningful way in the future, then they are fools
– absolute fools. I think Sam believes Paul and I have made
millions out of the stadium and retail park, he thinks we have
made his money in a way. He thinks we stepped into his shoes
and unfairly ousted him from the football club and the retail
park development.

Now we are completely out of the football club and the
retail park ourselves. We sold the retail park for just under
£60m to Aberdeen Asset Management. That got back most of
the loans made on the property. It was also the first time since
the project started that we had been paid a penny for the huge
amount of time we put in to making it happen.

I have to thank Vincent Tan for being a man of his word
in terms of the money we had put into the football club. The
people who acted on his behalf were very professional. He paid
up all the shares, for all the minority shareholders, meaning all
the people who put their money in to save the club – and who

had probably written it off – got it back. He could have left them there, but he wanted control. He also paid all the debts to PMG. For that reason we are extremely lucky because we could have been staring at a huge loss, but in the end we were fully covered.

Would we do it again? I am not sure. If we did then it would certainly not be for financial reasons. I think Paul in particular, as a director of Cardiff City, felt it was a chance to do something to help the club he supported. We were at serious risk there for a long time, having put that money in as the club's share of the deal, on the back of getting the revenue from the premium seating at the new stadium. We were meant to get that back in three or four months in theory, but of course we didn't. We have a huge amount of satisfaction over what we have all achieved, a massive pride when we see the stadium and retail park and think how nearly they did not happen, but we are not running round with 'Sam's millions'.

Anything that is happening with the stadium and the football club now is only possible because Sam was pushed out. I think he feels bitter he lost control of the whole thing at a critical time for him, but for me that was his own fault because he refused to listen, he wasted so much money over the years and still managed to pay Rudgwick's management fees. At the end of 2006 we thought we had finally seen the back of him. How wrong we were.

3

Rising from the Rubble

EVEN ONCE THE building work for the stadium and the retail park was up and running, there were many times I thought the whole project was going to collapse. It was always on a knife edge. It was still far from over the line, the project was not even on the home straight. On 16 February 2007, the outstanding matters included council approval, Welsh Assembly Government consent, plus the council's approval of the new arrangements with Sam Hammam and Rudgwick.

As an example of the daily highs and lows, I was on the train back from London when I had a phone call from Paul saying Laing O'Rourke had costed the design we had at £70 million to build the stadium. That was a problem because we only had £52 million available to cover everything, including huge fees. I just thought that was the end of that. Even in March 2007 they said the price of the stadium everyone wanted would be £47 million instead of the £40 million initially in the business plan. In April 2007, Paul Guy drew up a list of the four options available which was circulated to his fellow directors by email:

1) Abandon the project – even though £40 million is available, the land purchase is to be completed by the end of April, there are funds for athletics and the house of sport, the highways are finished, and the retail park has signed up Costco, ASDA and M&S.

If this is pursued then it is unlikely the club would avoid receivership due to the amount of money invested, £3 million plus the amounts owed to professional firms.

2) Reduce engineering costs.

3) Licensed shell option. Bare minimum to allow the public to watch football. Then use the stadium to gain extra funding through sponsorship and premium seating to fund the fit-out later.

4) Stadium redesign. New planning permission for 25,000 seater, 'unclear if club would survive such a delay.'

Our conclusion was to come up with a combination of options two and three. Peter's reply was: 'I agree it would be a disaster if after everything we fail to find a solution to this now. I think we need to agree our options before we drop the bombshell on Emyr [Evans, at Cardiff council]. We need to present him with the solution.' I replied: 'What can we build with £40m? If that is 20,000 seats and a three-quarter-finished stadium then so be it. That is easier to sell than a new planning application.'

Even at that stage, these were the discussions going on. On 13 April, Peter had a meeting with Cardiff council project manager Emyr Evans. The notes of that meeting record that PMG would guarantee the completion of the stadium. There would be a positive effect on employment as the project would create at least 800 jobs. Laing O'Rourke would give an undertaking the stadium would cost no more than £47.5 million, including £3.8 million for the fit-out. We were, perhaps optimistically, hoping to raise £15 million from debentures, plus we would try to reduce the costs further. Peter's notes of the meeting recorded: 'The loss of this project would cause untold carnage. The club's existence would once again be called into question. It is unlikely the current council leadership could survive.'

The project finally went unconditional in May 2007. Just three months later in August 2007, Northern Rock Building Society collapsed and it was the start of the largest economic crash in the UK since the Second World War. Wales in general and Welsh property prices in particular were among the hardest hit. We had no idea when the stadium project went 'unconditional' just how lucky we were and how close to the brink we had been. That deal would not have happened post-Northern Rock, there was too much financial uncertainty, property values had fallen too far to have any hope of making it viable – funding would have been impossible.

This whole experience was completely new to me. I had been involved in some pretty big property deals, but they were just property deals. This had plenty of extra elements as well as having to build an athletics stadium, the football stadium and retail park. There were all sorts of extra considerations, such as whether the stadium would be good enough for UEFA Championship events, where we would put the TV studios, how would the premium seating work, the roof design and even the pitch itself. For example we could not afford undersoil heating straightaway, so we decided to put the pipes in under the pitch ready and finish it later when we had the money from revenue generated by the stadium or the football club. Of course a rugby match was called off in that first season because of the cold weather and there was a lot of criticism, but that was just the way it had to be given the huge financial restraints.

There were plenty of problems, but we kept going for a variety of reasons. It was like being in a huge, slow-moving oil tanker that was impossible to turn. We had spent too much time and money not to want to see it go ahead. We had all invested money into the club for shares to replace Sam Hammam, we were only going to get that investment back if the club went to a new stadium. The other massive reason was that deep down we were Cardiff City fans and desperate for it all to succeed.

I had played rugby and still follow it closely, but I followed football as well. Cardiff City were my local club and I had always been interested. I was a regular watching them at Ninian Park, Paul and I wanted to see the club move forward. There was another key factor to consider. A temporary dispensation for keeping the standing terraces at Ninian Park depended on moving to the new stadium, so there was also a looming deadline which would have cut the capacity by 4–5,000. The ambitions we all had for the club would not have been viable if that had happened.

The outside world assumed that as soon as the project got the go-ahead from the council then the money would be available for the stadium and it would all proceed. However there was another huge element of risk. Ourselves and Capital and Regional were committing £35 million, so we needed enough commercial agreements to guarantee that we could go ahead and make the retail park workable.

We had agreements in place with retailers who had been waiting for years for something to happen. For instance wholesalers CostCo were involved from very early on, they were very keen to get a store open somewhere in Cardiff and they had a lot of other offers. It took plenty of trips to London to keep them warm, keep them informed and maintain their interest in taking the unit – essentially to reassure them the project would go ahead. All in all there were a lot of reasons why we felt that stadium simply had to get built.

The key element from the start, however, was identifying a food store. In some ways they would be the focal point of the retail park, so that was vital to the whole project. E J Hales, the Cardiff property agents, were very successful in managing to get Tesco interested. We agreed a lock-out period to secure a legal agreement with them and we had until 31 December 2005, to get that signed deal. Tesco were the only people we could talk to until after that date. They wanted a unit of 130,000 square feet, which would have required new planning permission.

Cardiff council were watching this proposed deal very closely. Also, once Tesco showed their hand, other operators suddenly became interested and we had competition. Other food stores like Sainsbury and ASDA were watching our progress with Tesco carefully and I knew that if we did not sign by the lock-out deadline then everything would be thrown into the air once more.

I felt a certain loyalty to Tesco and wanted to get the deal done. I phoned one of the main property directors at Tesco a few days before Christmas to tell him of the urgency, that I was willing to give up a holiday between Christmas and New Year and instead meet him in London to conclude the deal. He was at a Christmas party and was in no mood to turn his attention to this deal over the holiday period. They were overconfident; as it turned out they misjudged the situation terribly.

After the lock-out period expired, ASDA were ready to make their move. Critically they offered more money, £21.5 million, for a smaller store of 80,000 square feet for which we already had planning permission. It was more money per square foot and concluded the deal in ten days. We had thought ASDA would be the last people to be interested, because they have a huge store a mile and a half away in Cardiff Bay, but they were protecting their patch and also realised the potential in that area.

Tesco then went directly to Cardiff council offering £24 million. Tesco were offering more money, but for a 130,000 square foot store which would have required a new planning permission – as well as reducing the space available for the rest of the retail park. We were able to persuade the council it was better for the whole retail park to stick with ASDA.

On 31 January 2006, ASDA were officially announced as the proposed food store for the retail park. The front page of the *South Wales Echo* screamed 'IT'S A DEAL. ASDA huge new store boost to stadium plans as JCBs move in this summer.' BBC Wales described it as a 'watershed'.

I think now that if we had signed the deal with Tesco then the retail park would not have worked, there was not enough land left to put the money into the pot to make the rest of retail park happen and cover all the costs. If they had signed in time then we would have had to run with that, though. In hindsight we were lucky it worked out the way it did.

The next step was to choose the contractors to build the football stadium. McAlpine at first and then Laing O'Rourke showed strong interest. After the first round of meetings we thought the director from McAlpine had been the most impressive and we would run with them. It was a cheaper offer too, but in the second interview stage it became very clear that Laing O'Rourke would provide better value for money.

The over-riding reason for that change of mind was the performance and presentation by Laing O'Rourke board member Mike Lewis. Mike had been one of the important cogs in delivering the Millennium Stadium and his enthusiasm, knowledge and absolute confidence he could deliver was infectious. He is also a passionate Cardiff City supporter, the sort of character you would want alongside you in the trenches, someone we quickly realised would be a major ally in delivering the stadium. Due to the slight difference in initial prices, we had to persuade the council to go along with our decision. I think they too recognised that overall Laing O'Rourke gave value for money, with impressive professionalism and experience.

Once Mike Lewis got on board they were fantastic. They put a full team on it. They re-designed and value-engineered that stadium to a point where it could actually get built. Value engineering is a technical term for making compromises, doing things that work as well but cost a little less! It meant changing the design slightly, reducing the specification, to strip out costs, though of course any changes still needed to be approved by the council planners. It was a vital process we needed to go through. Without Mike Lewis and his team, who were all 100% committed, it would not have been possible.

There were still the usual games that are played between client and contractor. Anybody who has ever had any building work done knows the price usually creeps up. Steve Borley was a wonderful asset for the club during these days of negotiation. He is an astute businessman, he knew Mike Lewis and Laing O'Rourke well, and he was constantly arguing with them to cut costs but build more!

Alan Whiteley played a crucial role throughout in the negotiations with the council, who were certainly still worried about the state of the football club's finances and the possible impact on the overall project. At that stage the project had still not gone 'unconditional' so nothing was guaranteed. After a meeting on 11 April Geoff Shimmell wrote: 'Now the funding package does not work. Alan Whiteley mentioned the financial difficulties of the club yesterday in terms of the fees it owes and the risk of administration if the project isn't sorted out urgently.' Paul Guy replied: 'If the council view is to stop then I firmly believe the scheme will fail. Unless we go unconditional at the end of April this scheme will not happen.' He pointed out we would lose the retailers, the club was relying on reimbursement of fees and costs now totalling £3m, plus Laing O'Rourke needed to place orders for steel by 7 May to avoid a large and looming price increase.

We needed to plan to get the go-ahead, but the football club's financial position was worse than most people knew. Finance director Tony Brown sent an internal memo on 13 April 2007, forecasting a £2.7 million loss that year, a £4.7 million loss in 2008 and a £2.3 million loss 2009: 'The cash required to operate the business through to opening of new stadium is now £6.5m. The cash requirement to operate the business next season is £4m and the club will run out of cash in July 2007 despite repayments from unconditionality. There will no longer be any scope to manage cash flow through non-payment of Inland Revenue debts.'

Dave Jones and the team had managed to finish mid-table again, in 13th position, to preserve a place in the Championship which was also a crucial factor for our future. Off the field it was desperate, but there was some good news. We had been satisfying the requirements of the council one by one. Their professional officers looking at the numbers and the legal agreements were starting to report back to the chief executive that they were happy. At the beginning of May, Byron Davies wrote to confirm the council's willingness to assist with the stadium project. At last the scheme had gone 'unconditional', so in theory the funds were in place to complete everything.

After a tortuous afternoon in the council offices with all the lawyers present, signing dozens of documents, Cardiff council and the Welsh Assembly Government were now satisfied the necessary elements were there for a stadium up to 30,000 seats to be developed. There was £58 million committed to the stadium project, including all the different elements such as the athletics stadium and the House of Sport. That was made up of nearly £35 million from Capital Retail Park Partnership (PMG along with Capital and Regional), an estimated £9 million from the sale of Ninian Park (in the end this would be just under £8 million from Redrow Homes, but even then they had bought the land near the top of the market), £12 million from CCFC including PMG's shortfall loan of £9 million and a Football Trust grant of £2 million. Laing O'Rourke would build the stadium, Cowlin the athletics stadium and Carillion the House of Sport. This was backed by a £50 million funding facility from Principality Building Society for the retail park. Peter Ridsdale issued a press release:

> Two years ago this scheme was dead in the water, there were no retail tenants, a football club that was swamped in debt and a lack of confidence from the council that we could ever put together a credible business plan.
>
> I would like to go on record to thank everyone connected with Cardiff council, the developers Paul Guy and Mike Hall and Capital and Regional PLC, the professional teams at Laing O'Rourke and Principality Building Society that have put the designs, planning consents and funding together, and my colleagues at the football club for their contribution in making today possible.

A detailed schedule for the development was agreed, the athletics stadium had already started and work on the retail park got underway that month. The athletics completed in December 2007, the retail park was to open May 2008, work on the football stadium to start August 2007, to be completed March 2009, with Redrow starting the housing at the old Ninian Park ground in Spring 2009.

If that brought a feeling of optimism, just eleven days later

Tony Brown sent another internal memo about the cash flow position:

> We are unable to pay the Inland Revenue £344,000 as our full priority is on the players payroll which is due on 28 May. Our overdraft is £194,000. Given the recent interaction by the Inland Revenue with other football clubs, I am extremely concerned at their reaction to this non-payment.
>
> Our forecasts include the following assumptions – players payroll of £6.3 million, average attendances 14,500, £50,000 from the FA Cup. Birmingham retain Premiership status, £500,000 [from a bonus clause in the transfer of striker Cameron Jerome from Cardiff to Birmingham].
>
> The cash shortfall for next season is £4 million, there is no facility from Barclays as their policy is only to lend to Premiership clubs against fixed Sky income. I hope for an improvement in budgeted figures.

When the club transferred star striker Michael Chopra to Sunderland that August there was uproar from the fans. The fee was £2,352,000 initially from Sunderland, rising to a possible £4.5 million in total. Hopefully anyone reading this now will have a better understanding about why he had to be sold. When you look at the figures, there was no choice. Around 17 players were released that summer, though established stars such as Robbie Fowler, Jimmy Floyd Hasselbaink and Trevor Sinclair came in for the 2007/8 season. Some fans might substitute 'over-the-hill' for 'established', but you have to hand it to Peter Ridsdale and Dave Jones that they were able to attract such big names at the time.

When you do your financial planning, cash flows and business planning at a football club, you ignore all cup runs and try to make sure it can work without them. So anything the team did in the FA or Carling Cups was a massive bonus. We had drawn Tottenham in the FA Cup in 2007, drawing at home and losing 4–0 at White Hart Lane. Despite the defeat it was great for the club because we got a share of the away gate which came through within seven days – and it was a big cheque. It was also a lot of fun to enjoy the hospitality in the directors lounge at a Premier League club!

We were to have an OK season in the 2007/8 Championship, but the team beating non-League Chasetown at home in the third round of the FA Cup was a surprising start to a really important story. No-one was getting too excited when we beat Hereford away in the fourth round, at that stage we would have preferred a money-spinning defeat such as the year before against Tottenham. But then two early goals at home to Wolves meant a fairly nerves-free passage into the FA Cup quarter-finals and also meant we were one game from a Wembley semi-final. All we were asking Peter Ridsdale after every game was 'how much is it worth?' That money was literally keeping the club alive week to week.

After the draw for each round we would sit and sweat about whether we were chosen to be the TV game, because the big money kicks in with TV rights for live games. It is a sad thing to say because of the romance of the FA Cup and everything that goes with it in terms of history, but for us it was a numbers game – how far are we going to go and how much money is involved. The quarter-final at Middlesbrough was a live TV game. I was at home and I could not watch it, I was so nervous because we were one game away from a semi-final at Wembley. I was in and out of the toilet, in and out of the kitchen, going backwards and forwards, because we all knew how important it was financially to get to Wembley. For Dave and the players it was about the sport and the football side of playing at Wembley, but for people involved in the club's administration our attention was focused on how the money would get us out of a really big hole.

Two early goals in Middlesbrough meant we all went up to Wembley for the semi-final, where again the draw had been kind and we were up against Barnsley rather than a Premiership side. I took my two boys and we had a fantastic day. A goal by Wales international and Cardiff City youth product Joe

Ledley was enough to put us into the FA Cup final for the first time since Cardiff City famously won that trophy in 1927. We went into the changing room after the game and you could see someone like Steven McPhail had run himself into the ground that day. However it was amazing to think we would be going back and our tremendous supporters could enjoy another day out at Wembley. It was an enjoyable afternoon, especially being able to share a drink with such sporting greats as Dickie Bird after the game. Tony Blair's former spin doctor Alastair Campbell was also on my table at lunch, he was really interesting company.

In the FA Cup final we were up against Premiership opposition in Harry Redknapp's Portsmouth, with an extra million pounds of prize money for the winner. We may have lost 1–0, but more importantly that FA Cup run money was so vital in a lot of ways at a crucial time. It was disappointing to lose – and we could have won that game if things had gone our way – but it was such a great occasion. We watched the match from the Royal Box, Peter made sure Paul and I had enough tickets for family and friends, he gave us both signed Cardiff City shirts after the final. All in all it was a very memorable occasion despite the disappointment of defeat.

That year's FA Cup was worth a couple of million pounds overall, significant money to help pay the wages, pay the tax man and keep the club rolling forward. That was more important than romance, unfortunately. The 17-year-old midfielder Aaron Ramsey made an impression in that Cup run and he was bought by Arsenal for £5 million, another crucial step towards financial stability on the football side. Was it enough money for a player of his quality? Possibly not – but when you are broke, sadly your best assets get sold cheaply.

While the football club and the stadium development always had huge question marks hanging over them, the retail park is often assumed to have been much more straightforward. There are people who believe that as soon as it started we made millions – I wish that were the case, but it could hardly be further from the truth.

At one point there was a £50 million funding facility covering the retail park with the Principality, they were amazingly supportive of the project all along, especially through such a deep recession. There was £7 million estimated to cover the roads (it ended up being half as much again), plus £8,250,000 building the new athletics stadium, £3.5 million for the House of Sport, and so on. Steve Borley ultimately took responsibility for the House of Sport, he owns and runs it today – very successfully I believe!

There was even an issue over 40 nearby allotment holders using wells on the retail land to water their plants. Even though what they were doing was described as 'unauthorised and technically illegal' by the Environment Agency, we had to allow it because it was established practice. In the end it meant providing a new mains water supply to allotment holders, but it still took six months to sort out.

One key element was the support of major property company Capital and Regional PLC. The council may have been satisfied with all the conditions on their side of the deal, but on the other side was the retail park which was needed to make it all happen. All C&R were interested in was whether we could make that work financially. Supporters, players and the council all wanted new facilities, C&R just wanted a viable, profitable retail park.

In any large scale speculative development there is a tipping point where the number of tenants, retail tenants in this case, need to be signed up to underpin future value – and to justify the bank lending money. The key tenant to sign and the tipping point for this whole project was when Marks and Spencer exchanged contracts to take a large unit. Without them the stadium would not have gone unconditional in May 2007. Crucially this gave C&R and the banks the confidence that, together with CostCo, the health club and food store, that we had a viable project they could support. My gut feeling is that if M&S had not signed then we would not have had C&R or the Principality – and therefore no football stadium. Isn't it amazing to think that all the great days and nights experienced so far in that stadium would not have happened without one M&S unit.

Every day there was an issue we thought would trip us up, every day there was at least one email on some problem or other and there were a lot of times along the way when I thought we would have to throw the towel in because it was just too difficult. We were battling Hammam on one side, the council on the other, desperately trying to get a business plan done, persuading people in the council who did not believe we would get 14–15,000 people in the stadium every week, Laing O'Rourke were telling us there was not enough money to build the stadium (though they were helping as much as they could), C&R needed another tenant or they would not put in their part of the money. It was non-stop, we were continually juggling with a lot of balls up in the air, dropping any one of them would have brought everything down.

The council were also looking to get the sports village up and running in Cardiff Bay, so the likes of Toys R Us were encouraged to go down there, eventually we got Smyths Toys for Leckwith as a like-for-like alternative. I believe Smyths got the better end of that deal. As the people in the middle of it all, we were the only ones who knew just how many moving parts there were and how close to collapse it all was. For example Laing O'Rourke wanted around a million pounds to take responsibility for the risk caused by unexpected problems in ground conditions on the site. We did not really have that extra money, so we decided to take that risk as the developer because we had seen the ground reports and believed it would not be as bad as they feared. It could have been far worse than expected, but it ended up costing us £300,000 and that was another crucial saving, a calculated risk that worked.

The place was also covered in Japanese knotweed, a type of weed that has been classified as an 'invasive species.' It was difficult to get rid of and demolition firm Mike Cuddy did it with burner boxes, but that took time to get the Environment Agency and the council to agree because it was an uncommon way of dealing with it. It was difficult persuading the Environment Agency that would work compared to more expensive, but slower, solutions. All the time, there were these smaller problems cropping up to add to the bigger ones.

The council were blissfully unaware about how many difficulties that side of the development encountered. Any commercial element was rightly not of interest to the council, we had to take responsibility for any overspend, the roads and the contamination in the ground. There was a lot of risk on our side, which we did as much work as we could to mitigate.

There was a three- to four-month period towards the end of 2007 when it was certainly a fraught time. There were so many times I thought it would falter because there was a limited amount of money to build a stadium. Any overspend, for any reason, and the finances would collapse. Paul Guy adds:

> There were certainly three or four times that I thought it was definitely end of sports for this project. There was the Sam ultimatum day, we were also very close to finishing when Mike was able to extend the development agreement before it lapsed at the end of 2005. We had been trying to get Tesco but they did not commit, so we could not sign the development agreement. The council were very good on that occasion before ASDA came in. It was such hard work that everyone was getting a bit frayed at the edges and we wondered if it was worth it. There was a definite danger of 'deal fatigue', was it worth the effort?
>
> I have a saying now – one life, one stadium. It was the hardest thing we have ever done, we would never look to do something like that again. Looking back it was extremely difficult.
>
> Just before the Langston court case came up, I was driving to London in December 2007 and our lawyer Eamonn Cannon phoned me in the car. Peter Ridsdale was on the phone as well during that journey in quite a state. It appeared we did not have the security on our loan that we thought, if that was not all in place then we were really exposed – so that was a worrying time. I

thought that might be it then too. We are all glad it worked out in the end, but it was comfortably the hardest thing I have ever done in business.

Back in pre-recession 2007 we thought the retail park was going to fly financially once we started building it, we really did, we thought we would have no problem finding tenants. We had Costco, ASDA, M&S, so we did not think there would be any problems filling the rest.

The first time I really believed it was all happening was at a Cardiff City board meeting in the old Ninian Park and we were able to look across and see the steel work starting at Leckwith. It was quite exciting to watch the football stadium, the athletics stadium and the retail park come out of the ground. The athletics stadium is a fantastic replacement for the old facility, so the city of Cardiff has done well out of that too.

There was no time to relax, though. In 2008 the economy collapsed and the retail sector was one of the worst hit. Values plummeted and we had to buy out our joint venture partner Capital and Regional. We had £50m funding from Principality, so we had that level of debt on the retail park – arranged when the retail values and demand were high. When the crash came, the values dropped. In any banking agreement you have to keep your loan to value arrangement to a balanced level, so if the value drops the bank insist you drop your loan as well.

C&R thought there might be more of a financial demand on them to inject equity, so they were happy for us to buy them out of the retail park. We really struggled to raise the cash to buy out C&R from the retail park. I remember Paul and I approaching lenders and prominent wealthy individuals, but none were willing to back us. In the end a close friend of ours, Richard Crane, stepped in. The deal was sold to him in a chair lift on a skiing trip! He was also a key investor who helped to save the club.

There were a lot of risks and if that crash had happened a few months earlier then there is no way we would have been able to borrow money from the banks or get the retail value we needed to get the project up and running. It also made it far harder to get the final units filled. There is no question that the retail park was in intensive care for a long time. We had to battle at it, though slowly but surely we were able to do a few deals there. We were gently asked by the bank to sell the CostCo investment, which I regret doing but we had no choice. We sold it for around £17 million, which all went to paying off debt.

We put Les Croupiers casino in there, which was important at the time. You do not normally see a casino in a retail line-up but it was crucial rent to help pay the debts. They took a gamble (no pun intended) moving out of the centre of Cardiff, but the extra space seems to have worked for them. We did deals with Next and Smyths Toys for them to have shops there, but it took until 2012 to completely fill all the units. There was a long period of suffering and pain before we got to where we are now. We have been in it a lot, lot longer than we thought we would. Sometimes these things get sold before they are even finished and initially we were of a mind to do something like that here. However on this occasion it was a question of rolling up our sleeves, moving our offices down there and getting to grips with everything from service charges, security and car parking, as well as trying to attract tenants and just doing deals where we could.

Our journey with the retail park has only just come to an end and we have sold it to Aberdeen Asset Management. In the end, hopefully, the hard work was worth it. Neither myself nor Paul have directorships of the football club any more, so the only remaining link we have is going there to watch as Cardiff City fans. In the end the stadium project cost £53,441,316 to build. That was against a budget of £53,600,000, including all the loans, so it was brought in under budget by the tiniest of margins. That included the athletics stadium and House of Sport.

By today, that would all cost close to £100 million to build, so we had that one point in time when it could happen. I am not saying they would never have built a new stadium in Cardiff and reached the Premier League, but they would have missed the opportunity for at least a generation. Without the stadium, Cardiff City would not have a billionaire Malaysian owner now. They would probably have been playing MK Dons rather than Manchester United. It was massively important for Cardiff City that everything happened when it did. It was mighty close on countless occasions, but a large number of people helped to keep it on the right side of survival.

4

Court in the Middle

WHEN THE MONEY went into the Cardiff City Stadium account to confirm the whole project had gone unconditional in May 2007, Peter Ridsdale, Paul and I celebrated with a beer in the Park Plaza in the centre of Cardiff and I thought, 'Christ, this is really happening now.'

Two years of hard work, that felt like it had been for nothing on so many occasions, had finally paid off. Little did we know that the biggest threat of all was just round the corner in a very familiar guise. We thought we had seen the back of Sam Hammam in 2006 and kicked the Langston concerns into the long grass until 2016 when the stadium would be up, running and hopefully generating enough profit to pay him off. It would also almost certainly be someone else's problem by then as there was no way the current shareholders could be expected to run and sustain a Championship football club. We needed new investors with serious wealth.

We were getting on with things much better without Hammam and had made a lot of progress. We were concentrating on the details of the building work and filling the retail park, not knowing whether it would happen at all.

Just when we thought things had settled down, the future was thrown into turmoil as the mysterious Langston served writs on ourselves at PMG and also Cardiff City. That whole period was very traumatic. We had a lot of money tied up in the club, the stadium was underway and Langston were basically trying to wrestle control of all of it back again. It was particularly galling as we all thought, including Cardiff council, that Langston were happy with the re-negotiated package and they would now leave us alone in the important task of completing the stadium.

It was a worrying time, everyone involved in the stadium project was concerned it might all grind to a halt. We had to share our legal advice with the likes of Laing O'Rourke, the minority shareholders of Cardiff City and the council to help calm nerves.

I was on holiday in the summer of 2007 when the bombshell dropped and the writ was served from Langston, through their law firm Hextalls. I had it faxed through to me in Spain, a pretty lengthy document. At that stage I did not really understand the enormity of it and how much hassle it would cause. However if someone serves a writ on you it does concentrate your mind and set the hares running, you have to hire lawyers and litigation is a nightmare. It costs a fortune and is something to be avoided at all costs if at all possible. However we had no choice, along with the football club, we had to fight.

We were planning in terms of the club needing to pay Langston £15 million by October, 2016, as negotiated and signed by Sam Hammam at the end of 2006 as part of his exit agreement. We felt aggrieved enough about that because it was money Sam had spent in the first place, in our view unwisely, but the club would have to repay it to Langston or face administration. Suddenly, though, Langston were demanding £31,528,321 straightaway, or alternatively £16,680,370 each from Cardiff City and PMG. It was the original, secretive 2004 agreement between Langston and Hammam's Cardiff City, plus interest. They were arguing that none of the subsequent agreements with Sam were legal and so they counted for nothing. That simply was not possible, surely?

The first time we had a conference to discuss this, I was in the boardroom at Ninian Park with Peter Ridsdale, Steve Borley and Paul. We had David Wolfson, a barrister looking after our case, on the phone from London on a conference call. He basically said our position looked weak and we had a lot of work to do to defend ourselves. If we were going to lose the case then our money was at risk, around £11 million, so there was a real feeling of wondering 'What's going on here?'

The first part of Langston's case hinged on the Cardiff City Football Club board meeting of 20 September 2004, when Hammam told the other directors about the infamous loan notes from Langston that were needed to pay off the pressing debt to Citibank. In the second clause of that Langston agreement was a 'negative pledge' which did not allow anyone else to loan money to the club. It meant that, in theory, Cardiff City could not take out any more mortgages or borrow any more money from another source, such as when PMG covered the shortfalls on the stadium project. At the centre of the dispute was not whether that clause existed, because it did, but whether anyone still involved in the club or PMG knew about it when they were drawing up our arrangements.

That negative pledge would also put Langston first in line should anything happen to Cardiff City Football Club. Why was it so important to be first in line for debt repayment? Essentially that debt would be paid off before any other creditors, which meant they would always be in control of any administration process. Whoever was first in line would have the most powerful role in whatever happened next and in deciding who was appointed to look after the club. We felt the security we had on the £9 million shortfall funding meant we had first call on the business if it went bust, we had discussed how we would run it ourselves if need be to keep things going as best we could. However if Langston had won the court case they would have had both the first call and the ability to create that crisis situation by forcing the club into administration – a potential double whammy.

They were well aware of that likelihood and made it clear in documents sent by Hextalls: 'In the event the club goes into administration, Langston is willing to work with the council and any other necessary parties to complete the stadium project.' In other words they would step straight back in, now the project was up and running. Was that offer the key to the whole court action, revealing their true aim?

Initially they claimed Paul had been at that 2004 board meeting as one of the directors of Cardiff City at the time. Therefore he knew the full Langston loan note terms, including the negative pledge, so the reduction of the loan to £15 million and repayment extension to 2016 could be struck out as we had knowingly breached the terms of the previous agreement. The same applied to PMG's subsequent loan arrangements and security.

That was easy to disprove. As luck would have it Paul and I were in the Isle of Man on a Bentley-sponsored day which clashed with that 2004 board meeting. We had flown over in the morning, done some driving around in the Bentleys, played golf in the afternoon, had a big dinner in the evening and then flown back late. It was a very full and pleasant day, plenty of witnesses and documentation, not the sort of occasion you forgot in a hurry – and absolutely central to all the court action that nearly stopped the stadium development in its tracks.

Another clue should have been that Paul was marked down as absent in the handwritten minutes of that meeting, though as there were two versions of the minutes there was an element of ambiguity. Paul formally resigned as a Cardiff City director two weeks after that infamous board meeting in 2004, having become increasingly disconnected. He had been planning to resign for a while leading up to that point.

Langston were also claiming that the £24 million owed to them had gone towards funding the stadium development, though our records did not show any such evidence. Certainly none of that money was included in the business plan which had been agreed with the council and everyone else involved, while the accounts showed the bulk of that money being used to pay off the overdraft at Citibank.

Langston also argued PMG's susbsequent agreement on the £9 million loan to cover shortfall funding technically

THE MIKE HALL STORY

gave us control over the naming rights that had been offered
to Langston in 2006. On the face of it that may have been
correct because we were first in line for everything, including
the naming rights, but we would never have done that – we
always intended any naming rights would go to Langston as
agreed. I was always sceptical of the economic worth of the
naming rights for the stadium and thought their value was
significantly overplayed, so it was never a big issue to me. I
had a wager with Peter Ridsdale that I would run naked down
St Mary Street in the centre of Cardiff if he achieved this huge
figure. To this day no deal has been done on naming rights,
which perhaps is just as well!

The rest of the case was highly technical, or perhaps we
could use a simpler term 'absurd' – the word used in our court
submissions to describe their arguments. The agreement
drawn up with Hammam in 2006 depended partly on the
stadium project going 'unconditional' by 31 May 2007. If it
had not then in reality all bets were off and the club would
have gone into administration. It would not have mattered if
Langston were owed £15 million, £24 million or £30 million,
they would have been lucky to get tuppence ha'penny.

In fact the Conditional Development Agreement (CDA)
between Cardiff City Stadium Ltd and Cardiff council went
'unconditional' on 4 May. To make the deal happen, some of
the conditions had changed slightly by then. There were two
documents covering the 2006 arrangements with Langston
and in theory their validity depended on the CDA terms being
met. The first was described as 'The Deed', drawn up to cover
the terms of the original £24 million loan arranged with
Langston by Hammam, the second document was known as
'The Variation', to cover the involvement of the Devco, Cardiff
City Stadium Ltd, rather than the football club, the later date
of repayment and the repayment of interest – both documents
were prepared at the same time by Cardiff City lawyer Alan
Whiteley.

Alan was hugely influential behind the scenes, a brilliant

lawyer, very clever deal-maker, but also a Cardiff City fan. He put a huge amount of work into delivering the legal agreements and the legal strategy behind the whole deal. To this day he remains another unsung hero who helped save the club and make the new stadium a success.

That baffling phrase, the 'loan note variation' would haunt us. The Deed talked about the conditions set down by the council being 'satisfied or waived', as well as 'changed from time to time'. The Variation only talked about them being 'satisfied' and makes no reference to them being waived, varied or changed, in other words it was a more exacting test than in the Deed. Langston also argued that the Variation supplanted the Deed, rather than supplemented it.

It was a simple mistake, at most, in two documents drawn up at the same time that were plainly meant to be taken together. However it allowed Langston to claim that the 4 May agreement with Cardiff council giving the stadium the go-ahead did not 'satisfy' all the original conditions in the CDA and therefore did not apply under the terms of the Variation, even if they did meet the terms of the Deed.

It sounds complicated and it was, but as an example one of those changes involved the storage of the athletics equipment at the athletics stadium. It was not unreasonable to waive or change such conditions. It really was absurd to use stuff like that as reasons for bringing down the whole deal. Langston's submission was that those changes would have invalidated the CDA and therefore the 2006 Langston agreement (which reduced their debt to £15 million in 2016, plus proceeds from the naming rights). They claimed this opened the door to Langston demanding all of their money straightaway, plus interest, something they knew could only put the club into administration. Of course once the club went into administration they were prepared to help 'complete the stadium project'. I bet they were.

It would be fair to say trust was in fairly low supply. Apart from anything else Langston were arguing that PMG should be 'liable to Langston in damages for conspiracy to injury by unlawful means in the execution of PMG's debenture.' Langston were so confident of their case that they were not prepared to wait for a full court hearing, but went for a summary judgment – arguing the evidence was so clear cut in their favour it could be decided without a full hearing with witnesses. They took out High Court action against both Cardiff City and PMG, but only went for summary judgment against the club. That suggests two things – firstly that the action against PMG was on slightly shakier ground and secondly that their real target was getting control of the football club. Going for a summary judgment means testing the legal arguments alone because most of the facts of the case are agreed. In those circumstances there is no real need for a full court case with witnesses and cross examination to get at the truth. Strangely the two sides were in broad agreement of the facts, it was the impact and interpretation where we differed greatly.

The court case obviously put me in a very difficult position with Cardiff City, if it had gone badly there was a clear potential conflict between the interests of the club and PMG. I resigned from the Cardiff City board at the end of 2007 until this was resolved, but went back on in 2011 for a year until the Malaysians had taken over the club to move it forward again.

What were Langston after? On the face of it this case was about money, the return of £31 million, but Langston winning the court case would have sent the club into administration with huge debts so that money would not have been there to give them. Their best hope of getting some money back was to stick with the 2006 agreements, let the stadium and retail park get built and wait for £15 million by 2016 at the latest. By chasing £31 million in 2008 they were risking getting nothing at all.

However who controlled that process of going into administration was a central part of the court case and Langston made it very clear on several occasions they were

prepared to step back in to take over and 'work with' the club
and council to complete the stadium project.

If the 2006/7 shortfall funding of £9 million from PMG stood
the legal test then we would be in control of that administration
process and would not have let Hammam back in. If it did not
then he had an opening. Was Hammam prepared to gamble on
losing all those millions just to get back control of Cardiff City?
I wonder if he thought the prize of the stadium development
and retail park would be worth more than the £15 million that
he was still owed, or even the £31 million he was claiming. The
motives of Langston and Hammam, whatever the difference
between those two may be, are hard to understand, given the
terminal damage this court case could have done to the club.

Of course even with the Langston loan, Cardiff City had
run into financial problems, the stadium was stalling to say
the least in the summer of 2006 and if we had not stepped
in there would have been no stadium development. If Paul
had known about the negative pledge and stuck to the terms
that prevented anyone other than Langston helping the club
financially, Cardiff City would have gone bust there and then.
The new stadium and the rest of the development would simply
not have happened.

However there was another problem for us, a very big
problem. When we took out our security over the shortfall
loan, a clerical error by a solicitor meant it was not properly
registered. By the time this was rectified shortly afterwards
there was more of a claim we might have known the terms of
the Langston Loan Notes. When we first heard about the court
case from Langston we did not take it very seriously, but partly
because of that oversight it transpired it was potentially very
serious indeed.

Our loan had initially been arranged in October 2006, with
security against the premier seating debentures, three days
after Sam Hammam had agreed to dilute his shares and resign
as chairman. Because of his behaviour and agreement, we had
no reason to think of any 'negative pledge'. However those

original debentures became void, an omission that was spotted in December and therefore a second set of documentation was issued which was correctly registered and once again provided the security on our loans to the club. That security was finally registered properly in January 2007, well before we were made aware of Langston's claims the following summer.

Again we had no reason to think of checking for any negative pledge, nor knowledge of where to look, but the extra time meant there was more of an argument that we should have done. It was still a weakness in our case, probably our Achilles heel. On 6 February 2007, there was a Deed of Release which meant PMG had effective security under the January debentures. When the stadium project went unconditional in May that restated our loan of £9.2 million, the setting up of the Devco and our agreement using the Premier Seating debentures to pay us back.

There were many failed attempts to try and settle the case, but perhaps the most surprising happened in the most unlikely surroundings. I was on holiday in Dubai in January 2007, and was having lunch at a table next to the beach. I remember looking across at a nearby table and thinking I recognised Sam's lawyer from Hextalls – it couldn't really be him, could it? He was a larger gentleman and was clearly enjoying his lunch – he looked like a hundred others there, mostly from Russia, but it really was him after all.

Taking the opportunity, I went and said 'hello' and made polite conversation. I set up a meeting with him to discuss the case over a glass of wine, to see if we could figure out a way for all sides to avoid an expensive court case. We met him in the lobby of the Burj Al Arab hotel, a Dubai landmark built in the shape of a ship's sail and regularly voted the world's most luxurious hotel. It is one of the most iconic and recognisable buildings in the world... and most expensive, as we realised after two bottles of wine when we were once again left with an expensive bill – but no progress.

By October 2007, those legal hares were getting up to full

speed. We had responded to the initial legal documents, when Hextalls sent their reply on 12 October. It did not pull any punches and plenty of it was pretty personal. They argued the defence that we did not know the full terms of those loan notes, which had been waved around by Sam Hammam at that board meeting in 2004, was 'at best inaccurate and at worst a reckless statement which has no integrity. We contend there appears to be a distinct lack of integrity.'

It argued that, apart from anything else, a businessman of Paul Guy's calibre should have unearthed those terms by doing due diligence before loaning £9 million. In conclusion it said: 'It appears from the above that Paul Guy, Peter Ridsdale, Mike Hall and maybe others have not been entirely candid with the information that ought to have been disclosed.' We felt we were being called liars. We also felt that being candid was something that could work both ways. Hextalls, on behalf of Langston, denied Hammam was 'evasive about his connections with Langston.' They did however admit by now it was a mistake to say Paul was present at the meeting in 2004. Their letter said:

> The claimant's case (Langston) is that both Defendants (Cardiff City and PMG) executed the debenture (our shortfall loan) knowing and intending that it would give the Second Defendant (PMG) in breach of contract rights by way of security superior to those of the claimant.
>
> The claimant will say that in certain respects identified in this reply, Peter Ridsdale and Paul Guy could not truthfully have stated that they believed the facts stated by the defence to be true.

In other words it was accusing ourselves and Cardiff City of knowingly breaking the terms of the Langston loan, which none of us had been involved in arranging or approving, or indeed had we ever read a copy until the start of the court action. Quite strong claims to say the least, but could they back them up?

As evidence they put forward the minutes of the meeting of

the board of directors of Cardiff City Stadium Ltd on 31 August 2006. Those at the meeting were Paul Guy, Ned Hammam, Peter Ridsdale and myself, along with lawyers James Dakin to advise PMG, and Alan Whiteley to advise the football club. The loan notes were discussed, including some of the terms and conditions, and that was recorded in the minutes. We were trying to persuade Ned and Sam Hammam to accept the reduced terms of the Langston loan notes to £15 million to satisfy the council and the business plan. If they had agreed that would allow the stadium development to go ahead, of course there was nothing recorded in the minutes about a negative pledge being discussed because it was not mentioned.

There were also the minutes from the original meeting in 2004, or at least one version of them. Paul was still a director at that stage and did receive the minutes afterwards. If Hammam had shown the details of the 2004 loan notes to the directors, or recorded all the terms clearly in an unambiguous set of minutes of the meeting, then we should not have carried out our future dealings to save the stadium. There was an email that included some of the terms, but Paul did not read it all because he was in the process of ending his involvement in the football club – not least because of the way Hammam was running it.

It did not help that there were two versions of minutes from the meeting. David Temme's contemporaneous, handwritten notes do not suggest the details were explained by Sam, while other conversations and discussions between the directors at the meeting are recorded. The 'official' minutes were signed by Hammam and obtained during the early stages of the court case in late 2007 from the offices of Hammam's lawyer Peter Lloyd Cooper. They include great detail about the Loan Notes, including the negative pledge, but no mention of any conversation or discussion between the directors at the meeting. They seemed to have been drawn up by someone who was not present at the meeting and differed from the eye-witness accounts, so we did not consider them a completely reliable record of events shall we say! David Temme recalled in information provided for the court:

> I did not prepare the formal minutes and did not circulate the formal minutes or copies of the Loan Stock Agreement to the directors.
>
> The other directors also had no input into the terms of the Loan Stock Agreement and in all respects it was a fait accompli when it came to the board for 'rubber stamping'.
>
> I also do not believe it was the only option available to the club prior to its adoption but it probably was at that moment in time as SH [Sam Hammam] would not consider any other structures and time had run out with Citibank.
>
> I know that the Agreement signed by me remains undated and the 'official Agreement' was signed and dated by Sam Hammam and Peter Lloyd Cooper [Hammam's lawyer and the club lawyer at that time]. Why would that be?
>
> The other directors did see the document at the board but they did not have copies and they did not have an opportunity to consider the implications of the whole or part of the Agreement save what was presented to them by SH on the face of the document.
>
> The only people who understood the details of the document were Sam Hammam and Peter Lloyd Cooper and ALL details were finalised pre-board and the board had no input or room for debate in the process.
>
> SH considered that as the owner of 82.5% of the shares of the club/company he did not need to report to or to discuss any of his actions with others. In this regard, it is perhaps difficult for people to understand that meetings were often simply a collection of people in the same room as SH listening to him speak/dictate what he wanted. This extended to the advisors meetings and I have little doubt that SH never saw any reason why directors would need to understand or be part of the Loan Stock Agreement save when he needed their money to prop up his expenditures.

Paul Guy takes up the story:

I was not there but the other directors are very clear that negative pledge was never put in front of the board. Sam just said there was the money, he had signed it. There never was any discussion of any negative pledge in there.

When we were putting all our money in at a later stage, it should have been very clear to Sam we were only doing this if we had a first legal pledge on that money. He never mentioned the negative pledge then, he accepted and signed all of that.

The judge made the point no-one would put this sort of money in, as we did, unless you had first legal charge against the debt.

It was only afterwards they tried to allude that I knew the details, but not only did I miss that meeting but not one of the directors knew.

Sam argued that we could have grabbed 'his' naming rights, which in theory we could have done, but we would never have done that and were happy to carve that out. He would always say we had his naming rights, but that was never our intention.

We would have been happy to sit down and let him have anything he was entitled to, the naming rights or the money if Cardiff City were promoted, he could have all that.

Peter Ridsdale mentioned to the press that Cardiff City could go into administration because of the court case. On 21 November, Hextalls sent a letter questioning PMG's right to appoint that administrator: 'We are prepared to discuss ensuring sufficient funds are available to enable the administrator to continue trading at the club.' They were happy to put up money to take control of that process, then, which was interesting.

They had also asked for Langston to have representation on the Cardiff City board once again. We replied on 22 November saying that was 'entirely unacceptable to offer Mr Hammam or Langston a position on the board.' It pointed out that the 2004 loan note 'engineered by Mr Hammam was patently unsustainable and the club's demise was imminent but for the renegotiation.' The 2006 agreement was recognition of what the club was able to do, but we were happy to look at accelerating repayment and some of the other terms if the court action was dropped.

The following day a strictly private and confidential briefing note outlined the legal structure that now applied to the Cardiff City Stadium. It explained that the Devco had been set up before the Langston court case, it was needed for several reasons: because Cardiff Blues rugby club did not want the football club as owner of the ground in case of clashes, PMG would not release funds to club in 'the light of current developments', selling seats had proved difficult, while adverse publicity from the Langston court case meant loss of confidence in the club. In other words CCS had not been set up to cut out Langston, there were other driving forces, but the seriousness of the situation and the damage the court case was causing the club could not be underestimated.

Hammam was also doing well in the publicity war, with some fans who felt a loyalty to him for kick-starting their bigger dreams for the club. We felt the fans were paying too much attention to his professed passion for Cardiff City and we should issue something to put the facts straight. We prepared an open letter to send to the press and fans, though eventually it was never released as we decided to keep our powder dry for the court case. We can reveal it now:

If Langston wins the current court case against Cardiff City Football Club the club will go into administration. That is company law set down by Companies House.

We loaned the club £3m under the Sam Hammam regime. We have turned our loan into a sponsorship deal. We rescued the scheme when the previous regime under Sam Hammam was unable to make the stadium a reality and were saddled with £2m of unpaid professional fees.

Langston Corporation is a Panama registered company and the two directors are not individuals but two British Virgin Island companies. Sam Hammam has conducted all negotiations on behalf of Langston.

In October 2006 an agreement was signed with Langston that reduced the loan notes from £24m to £15m and deferred payment of interest and capital until 2016. In lieu Langston were granted naming rights for the new stadium, all subject to the stadium becoming 'unconditional'. Otherwise the club faced immediate insolvency proceedings.

Langston argued 'unconditionality' had not been met by 4 May 2007 and therefore all the £24m is repayable. We have had no human contact with anyone apart from their solicitors Hextalls and Hammam. Behind the scenes Hammam is trying to wrest back control of the club. PMG will not entertain Hammam returning after creating the financial meltdown and now trying for a second time to bring the club down. Hammam is trying to renegotiate the deal that saved the club.

Without that deal it is difficult to see how the club can avoid having to appoint an administrator. They seem to want to destroy the club and end up with very little of their debt being repaid.

It was a pretty good summary. However while the publicity war was important, the legal battle was much more crucial. On 4 December our lawyers Nabarro sent a letter to Langston explaining: 'The present claims are putting the club under enormous financial strain. The interruption of income streams to the club, caused by the litigation, is likely to have imminent fatal consequences for the club and therefore for Langston as an unsecured creditor.'

That made the situation crystal clear. We also asked to meet Hammam the next day, though that did not happen. We tried to come up with other solutions. On 21 January in a draft heads of agreement we suggested the Langston debt be agreed at £15m plus interest from 1 March 2007, the balance to be paid by October 2016. Naming rights at the new stadium of up to £9.3m would go to Langston. Langston would rank second behind PMG in repayment. All litigation would be terminated. Any sale of CCFC for more that £45.5m would see repayment for Langston.

As an example of the seriousness of our situation it would take Langston just 50 minutes to win the next round in court. They were worried we would put the club into administration as a way of getting round the court case, so they got an injunction in less than an hour on 5 February 2008 to stop us. In fact administration was a last resort because of the jeopardy it would have caused the stadium project and Cardiff City's future on the field. We were not present at the hearing, but were informed afterwards that if we put the club into administration and appointed an administrator that: 'If you, PMG Estates Ltd, disobey this order you may be held in contempt of court and fined or have your assets seized.' We would have the chance to overturn that at future hearings, though.

This was all about Langston and Hammam trying to get control back – and they had a genuine chance. The way Hammam's lawyers Hextalls were putting pressure on in every way was clever and superficially persuasive. If you read their case on paper, without knowing both sides, then it appeared to be a strong argument.

We were working on the basis, as advised by our barrister David Wolfson, that we were in danger of losing the case, that they may have found a loophole. I think he told us that to make sure we were ready to really work hard with him to get all the information so he could put the case together. He was fantastic, a top, top bloke. For the next six months before it went to court, Paul and I had conference calls with him in all sorts of places – for instance we were over in Paris for the weekend watching rugby, but still taking conference calls in the hotel rooms. It was really hard work, sitting with lawyers going through everything. It took hours and hours and cost hundreds of thousands of pounds to defend this action.

We went to a huge amount of effort to settle this with Langston, with numerous trips up to London to spend hours sat in meetings with Hammam and his advisors. We tried everything on our side, the club and PMG. There was a lot of to-ing and fro-ing with lawyers involved, some meetings lasted five minutes because he got up and walked out while some lasted for hours.

In February we tried to come up with a deal that would give Langston at least £10 million sooner rather than later, depending on whether the club was sold, the potential income from the naming rights or a possible hotel or residential element of the redevelopment. Langston still insisted on having a director on the Cardiff City board. There were so many such stumbling blocks and so in the end we ran out of options and the case went to court.

When that day came Peter Ridsdale and I travelled up to the High Court separately, Paul was on holiday. I got dropped outside the High Court around 200 yards from the entrance. I saw a huge scrum of photographers and cameras and thought there must been something else big going on that day, surely that wasn't for our case? Then the cameras turned and pointed at me as I walked into court and the seriousness of the situation hit me.

Because the lawyers had not initially properly registered our security, if the club went bust we were in potential difficulty. We had taken a second opinion from Lloyd Tamblin QC which was faxed through to me at the end of the first day of the court case. When I read it I went cold because the advice was that if we lost the court case we were in trouble and that spooked me. Phrases like: 'We are in my opinion in uncertain legal territory', were not comforting. Not only would we have lost the money, but the club would have gone into administration. That was not an easy way out, we realised how damaging administration would be for the club, losing league points, losing players and probably being relegated.

If we had security, then if Langston won the case they could not really do that much. They could try to fold the club, but then they would have had to talk to us because of the security in place. If we did not have first security then this was serious, we were in danger of losing all our money and any involvement in the stadium project. Cardiff City would be back in Langston's hands, or their 'representative' Hammam, for them to do what they wanted with it. It did not bear thinking about.

We had asked whether we could withhold the £9 million if we lost the case, the answer was that would be very difficult.

We wanted to know if our security was solid, but Lloyd Tamblin felt Langston had an arguable case if they could show we knew about the loan note documents. They could get an injunction to rule out our second debenture agreement, the one which was properly registered. We had no chance of putting any new security in place as by definition at this stage of the court case we knew all about Langston's negative pledge in the original loan notes. Lloyd Tamblin summed up: 'The claim raised by Langston in the proceedings cannot be dealt with other than by establishing that it is misconceived.'

We had to win the court case, or else, but how do you prove a negative? We had to prove we did not know about the negative pledge in the loan notes – and how to do that was not the $64,000 question; it was a multi-million pound question.

I had not planned to stay up in London, but this was obviously so serious I went and booked a hotel room and stayed for the rest of the case. I sat there next to Peter Ridsdale and behind David Wolfson, who is a brilliant legal mind. He made complex legal arguments seem understandable and put them into plain language. It was a fascinating experience seeing all that going on at the High Court, if not a little nerve-wracking, though I did get told off by David Wolfson during lunch on the first day for nodding so enthusiastically every time the judge said anything I agreed with.

Hammam was never there, he did not show his face once. Langston's barrister was very good at the written word and putting their case that way, but I felt ours was better on his feet in the court. At the end of the first day he was given 20 minutes to start summing up our case. He made a big point of pointing out the empty seats where representatives of Langston should have been sitting. Who were these people, why would they not show their faces?

It was easy for us to prove that Paul was not at that 2004 meeting, it was also fairly easy to show that none of the directors knew the detail of that Langston loan – that was not Hammam's style. The eye-witness evidence from David

Temme and Steve Borley made that very clear. It was also relatively straightforward to show that we did not know about the negative pledge in 2006 and even the start of 2007. There was that second area where Langston attacked us – the Deed and the Variation. Alan Whiteley had prepared both and his evidence read:

> I thought at the time the easiest approach was to draft two documents. This was entirely driven by technical considerations and the logic of the documentation: the commercial agreement reached was a single agreement; it would not have made any sense to divide the commercial agreement and the division in documentation was for drafting reasons only. The two documents taken together represented the single, integral agreement actually reached.
>
> Langston's construction flies in the face of the whole commercial logic of the situation. What Langston now pleads would not have satisfied the council and allowed the project to continue. To construe the documents in the way Langston pleads produces a result which is arbitrary and absurd.

We had another piece of crucial evidence in our favour. The Langston loan note theoretically prevented the club taking out any mortgage or borrowing from any other source after 2004. However Hammam had been so desperate for money on at least three other occasions, that he had broken those terms himself. Not only did he not reveal those terms to the other directors, he did not even abide by them in his own dealings. There were three loans, starting with one from the Professional Footballers Association to pay the players' wages in early 2005. Peter Ridsdale's submission reported:

> Sam had put the PFA loan in place after the Loan Notes and the PFA loan was secured. It therefore did not occur to me that there would be any negative pledge in the Loan Notes. I also assumed that, since Sam always said about the Loan Notes, 'Don't worry, they are unsecured,' that there would be no negative pledge. Sam signed a personal undertaking not to violate the charge put in

place in favour of PMG Estates Ltd. Actually Barclays also had a
fixed and floating charge on season ticket monies passing through
them, which I also had to get released to allow the club to trade.

There were therefore three occasions in 2005 when Sam [who
is or represents Langston] agreed to secured borrowing after the
Loan Notes were issued, and in breach of the negative pledge: with
the PFA in February 2005, Barclays in the summer of 2005 and
then with PMG Estates in December 2005.

That meant that proving the close connection between Sam
Hammam and Langston would make it a pretty open and shut
case, barring something remarkable. For the many reasons
explained already, that was not too difficult to do.

As the evidence unwound you could see that there was
no real way we were going to lose it. David Wolfson was an
extremely intelligent QC, but I remember him telling me there
was clear blue water between his intellect and that of Justice
Briggs who was presiding over the case. That was a scary
thought for a Land Economy student, who was already in awe
of David's intellect! The judge grasped all the documentation,
all the nuances, all the things that were going on with Langston
and Hammam, why they were bringing the court case – he got
it all.

Waiting for the verdict was still a nervous time. The night
before the final verdict the judgment was sent to our lawyers,
Nabarro. However they would not tell us the result, they
totally embargoed it. They would not even give us a hint or
any indication at all. I was on the phone to them and asked
them to stay silent for ten seconds if we had won, or just tap
the phone, anything to give some indication, but they would
not.

When we all went back up to London, we filed into court
and stood there waiting for the judgment – you could feel the
tension. We won it hands down and we won costs as well.
Justice Briggs was only hearing the summary case, about
whether the legal arguments held enough water to justify going

further, but he went so far as to suggest any further action on the case would have very little chance of going Langston's way. He effectively dismissed their case.

Justice Briggs was very firm on the main part of Langston's claim: 'I have reached the clear conclusion that this is not a case for summary judgment because on the assumed facts the club has a very real prospect of a successful defence. The club's evidence discloses a real prospect that it will be established at trial that Langston's governing mind and will at all material times was that of Mr Sam Hammam.'

Justice Briggs said that without the agreement which saw Hammam leaving Cardiff City, the club had faced likely insolvency and Langston would have only got a 'modest proportion' of the debt. Langston had a choice between that or accepting the smaller repayment and longer time scale. He pointed out that Hammam knew all about the arrangements for the Devco, after all his brother Ned was on the board in the early days. He did nothing to step in and enforce the negative pledge.

Legal precedent was on our side that the Variation added to the Deed, rather than replaced it. For the law students amongst you: Saunders v Ralph and Morris v Bacon! Justice Briggs was clear the two documents were intended to go together, so the clauses of the Deed would also apply to the Variation: 'It seems to me that the intention that there should be no more than a variation of the CDA [Conditional Development Agreement with the council] puts the issue beyond doubt in favour of the club.' He also made it clear that all this was known to the 'relevant governing minds of Langston [Mr Hammam and Mr Tischhauser].' Justice Briggs did more than he was asked in a summary judgment and 'concluded' that the Variation did not terminate the Deed and invalidate the CDA.

He also concluded the waiver of certain conditions covered all parts of the agreement with the council, not least because that was so plainly the intention of all those involved. Again Justice Briggs went further than necessary by adding that he would expect the club to succeed in proving these arguments, though Langston still had the opportunity to try to establish something different at a full trial.

We had won on every level and were even awarded costs to underline that victory. Being awarded costs was a bit misleading as even after that we were substantially out of pocket, but it was a clear additional statement about who was right and who was wrong. Hammam and Langston have been on the back foot since that court case.

It was all so unequivocal it was fantastic. It was a relief as well, because the summary judgment was unusually heavily in our favour. It was a vindication. You have this burning feeling inside you about the injustice of it all, the case that has been brought, the person or people bringing it, and everything that go with that. You never know that everyone else is going to see that, so for the final verdict to be the way it was nailed on my faith in the justice system. For Justice Briggs to understand it so brilliantly and deliver the judgment he did was still a relief.

It brought out similar emotions to winning a big match. When you are involved in a sporting contest then it is fantastic to win, but winning this court case was right up there because we were so heavily tied in. We had gone into this stadium scheme with good intentions, but in the end we had gambled so much to make sure it happened and here we were staring down the barrel of a gun. We had never envisaged this, we had held out the olive branches so often to try and resolve the action but every time we were refused. After all that, it was a nice vindication to see Langston and Hammam getting so completely defeated.

We all went out and celebrated at a nice restaurant in Mayfair that Peter Ridsdale organised. It was a massive relief to everyone to have won, even though it still cost the club and us hundreds of thousands of pounds. Whenever Hammam purports to care about Cardiff City Football Club it is worth remembering how much money he cost the club at a time it could not really afford it – money that should have been spent on players!

As a side issue, Hammam's law firm Hextalls went into administration a few months later blaming cash flow problems. I wondered if our case was partly responsible for that, though there may have been other contributory factors. They are back after a takeover, trading on a firm footing now.

My opinion is that Langston is Sam Hammam, as Justice Briggs put it he is the "relevant governing mind," and I have no doubt about that – even though we have no proof. What annoys me, though, is that he lost all that money. He spent it and lost it chasing his football dreams of promotion. He was not the first and he will not be the last person to lose money in a football club. He was paying big wages and bonuses when others might have been able to drive harder deals. I believe that after his success with Wimbledon he believed he was untouchable. He had no-one other than himself to blame as he ran the club in an autocratic manner.

You cannot deny he did massive things right for Cardiff City, perhaps he just got carried away and realised too late the enormity of the problems he had created.

He has seen a return of at least some part of the loan under new owner Vincent Tan, along with the title as Life President. There had to be a deal or a full repayment at some stage, the only other option was for the club to go into administration and start again. I sometimes wonder if we should have done that, but we would not be where we are now if we had. It would certainly have delayed everything, if you go into administration it takes years to recover. The club had been exposed to that risk for years, it was only when the Malaysian Tan Sri Dato Seri Vincent came in as owner of Cardiff City that you felt he had the financial wherewithal to sort it all out.

Even in 2012 Hammam was trying to reclaim his total money, with interest, to put the club into administration and work his way back in. Of course had he been successful then there would have been no promotion to the Premier League.

Any fans who still pay attention to his claims should remember that. Crucially, Langston's new lawyers Walker Morris wrote on 2 October 2012:

> Langston has claim against CCFC [Cardiff City Football Club] to redeem each of the 24,000,000 units of stock held by LGC [Langston] at a rate of £1.30 for each unit together with interest. If CCFC is not prepared to repay monies owing to LGC, LGC are in a position to place CCFC into administration.
>
> Our clients are also aware of several other parties who would be interested in purchasing CCFC from the administrators in the event CCFC entered administration. LGC's position is that all debentures granted subsequent to the original loan note are invalid and that CCFC has been insolvent for some time. As all debentures registered against CCFC were subsequent to the original loan note, that Langston is the first priority creditor over CCFC.

It was the 2008 court case all over again, with no reason to believe there would be a different outcome this time round. We were fairly relaxed and the club sent a very strong rebuttal. However there was also a new – and much more personal – dimension to this threat. The letter went on:

> Should CCFC be placed into administration then there will be personal ramifications for the directors and shadow directors. We will ensure that an administrator/liquidator will take all steps to pursue all of those individuals in their personal capacity for misfeasance pursuant to section 212 of the Insolvency Act 1986.
>
> In addition to the civil claims outlined above, any directors will be susceptible to disqualification processings initiated by the Secretary of State. This could result in disqualifications from being directors for as much of 12 years.

Safe to say he really does not like Paul and myself, and almost certainly thinks we are running round with money he considers 'his'. He is wrong on so many levels, but while we were genuinely concerned in 2008 and the court case is something none of us would want to go through again, we are very confident that there is no longer any legal threat to fear from Langston. The money being paid to PMG was simply a very slow repayment of the shortfall loans which allowed the stadium project to get off the ground.

Now it seems the Langston deal has been sorted out and re-paid – at least in part – by Vincent Tan as the owner of the club and its liabilities. We do not think Hammam deserves a penny after he spent that money in the first place, as well as the cost and concern Hammam and Langston have put the club through since. However at least, and at last, it seems to have been resolved as an issue.

The Langston loan was an unsecured loan; the naming rights for the stadium have never been sold. There were ongoing weaknesses in Langston's position and hopefully Vincent Tan and his advisors used those to good effect to keep the costs down.

Whatever Cardiff City fans feel about their new owner, and the details about wearing red or blue shirts, he has done a great service to the club in resolving the Langston issue once and for all. It has weighed heavily on the club for almost a decade, a millstone holding the club back.

5

Ridsdale's One-man Band

THE DAY AFTER Cardiff City reached the Premier League in May 2013, I heard an interview with Peter Ridsdale about the transformation of the club, the new stadium and the subsequent return to the Promised Land. He took a lot of the credit for the new stadium and the transformation without mentioning anyone else as having played a part. In his book, *United We Fall*, the section on Cardiff City does not mention a single other name of anyone who helped turn the club round. 'Investors' are mentioned, along with Sam Hammam's efforts at getting rid of a 'Ridsdale-led board', but that is it.

I was disappointed and a major incentive to publish this book of course is to set the record straight on behalf of the many people who played crucial roles. Peter played a part, but the new stadium and turnaround in fortunes might well have happened without him. There are quite a few architects of this project, without whom Cardiff City would not be playing at a new stadium having enjoyed a season in the Premier League. There are plenty of people who deserve huge recognition for their vital contributions.

First and foremost – without Paul Guy's work ethic and attention to detail it would not have happened. He really got stuck into this and got to grips with it. At one stage we were dealing with around 200 emails a day at PMG just about this project. Paul's aptitude for dealing with this, sitting in front of the council scrutiny committees, dealing with the politicians – it was his ability, business acumen, perseverance and belief which got this built.

Steve Borley played an equally important business role, but more importantly he also played a key practical role in the delivery of this project. I think at one point he was working full-time on this with only the best interests of the club as a reward. He worked tirelessly to keep Laing O'Rourke on track and to make sure they delivered as good a stadium as possible for the money available. He had got the ball rolling back in 2000 by starting discussions with the council and he played a huge part in pushing it over the finishing line, while remaining involved all the way through.

Mike Lewis from Laing O'Rourke – we would never have got it done without him. Because Laing's had lost so much money on building the Millennium Stadium, he could have been forgiven for turning his back on another huge stadium project in Cardiff. Instead he went out on a limb and said he would get it done on budget. I remember Mike saying at the very beginning: 'We are at the start of the Grand National, we have 28 fences to get over and they will keep getting higher. If we do not work together then we will never get over them.'

Paul Norman, the project manager during the building of the stadium, is a massive Cardiff City fan so it was a real labour of love for him. He moved heaven and earth to make it work and build a quality stadium for the future, along with his team. Of course they were doing their jobs and getting paid, but they all went the extra mile. There was a big feeling in that team that they were going to make it work, they would find engineering solutions if something was too expensive, find alternative ways of doing things, redesign where necessary, re-tender – whatever was needed. That whole professional team from Mike Lewis at the top through Paul Norman to the rest of them had an attitude that they could get it done – which was quite powerful. They were massively important.

Planning lawyer Philippa Cole went through around 200 planning consents on this site. The late David Temme, the former Cardiff City chief executive, played a huge role in the initial stages and without him it would have withered on the

Going past Ireland centre Brendan Mullin on the way to victory over Oxford in my first Varsity Match at Twickenham. The following year caused controversy when I chose to play for Cambridge in the Varsity Match instead of playing for Wales

Tackling Scotland full back Gavin Hastings, he was a predecessor at Cambridge and one of the reasons I chose to go there

© Huw Evans Agency

Sharing a joke with Ieuan Evans at Wales training
© Huw Evans Agency

Llanelli playmaker Nigel Davies and I formed a good centre pairing in the year Wales won the Five Nations Championship under coach Alan Davies
© Huw Evans Agency

In action for Wales against Scotland – for some reason I usually played well against the Scots

© Huw Evans Agency

Former Wales rugby coach Alan Davies – he had plans in place for the 1995 Rugby World Cup but never got the chance to put them into action. He succeeded in bringing the Wales squad together and resolving club rivalries

© Huw Evans Agency

A try for Cardiff
against Swansea – I
was happy really
© Huw Evans Agency

Lifting the Schweppes
Cup trophy at the
National Stadium
alongside wing Steve
Ford, with Prince Charles
and Sir Tasker Watkins
looking on – it does not
get much better than
that. And we had beaten
Llanelli in the final…
© Huw Evans Agency

In action for Cardiff – I felt I played some of my best rugby after retiring from internationals in 1995

© Huw Evans Agency

Being appointed Wales captain for the 1995 World Cup meant having to face the press. It was controversial maybe, but who would have turned down the offer?

© Huw Evans Agency

Cardiff against Neath – eventually we found a way of beating the Welsh All Blacks

© Huw Evans Agency

An artist's impression of what the Cardiff City Stadium would look like – we got pretty close with the end result

The front of the Cardiff City Stadium during construction – even after the building work had started we still faced many problems. This was the view from beside our offices in the middle of the development

The Stadium business plan we put forward to Cardiff council on the left, the one prepared under Sam Hammam on the right. Guess which one was accepted?

Former Cardiff City owner and chairman Sam Hammam – quite simply the most impossible man I have ever had to deal with in business

© Huw Evans Agency

Former Cardiff City chairman Peter Ridsdale watching alongside fellow director Steve Borley. They both made big contributions, but they were also part of a big team

© Huw Evans Agency

Owner Vincent Tan has put many millions of pounds into Cardiff City, that gives him the right to make some unpopular decisions. However I am sure he would not have got involved in Cardiff City, providing the money which got us into the Premier League, if we had not built the Cardiff City Stadium

© Huw Evans Agency

Manager Malky Mackay celebrates the 0–0 draw with Charlton that sent Cardiff City up to the Premier League. I think he would have kept Cardiff City in the Premier League if he had been given the chance

© Huw Evans Agency

The best day in the Premier League as Cardiff City beat Manchester City 3–2 at the Cardiff City Stadium – it was the sort of occasion that made all the hard work worthwhile. Aron Gunnarsson celebrates the first goal with watching fans

© Huw Evans Agency

Fraizer Campbell scored the decisive third goal as Cardiff City beat eventual champions Manchester City in the first Premier League game at the Cardiff City Stadium
© Huw Evans Agency

The group that climbed Mount Kilimanjaro, the highest peak in Africa. Everyone looks pretty relaxed, including 15 former Wales rugby captains, but there was a long way to go

The calm before the storm – getting ready for the final push to the top the following day. The peak behind us doesn't look that hard – but it was

There's only one top of a mountain and this was the group who made it. There was some emotion when we got to the peak, it was one of the hardest things I have ever done

© Huw Evans Agency

Welsh photographer Huw Evans organised the expedition and played a key role in raising hundreds of thousands of pounds for Velindre Cancer Care

© Huw Evans Agency

All the fundraisers who completed the Boston to New York cycle ride. This is just one part of the efforts which have raised £13 million for Velindre Cancer Care over the last five years

Former Wales rugby players Martyn Williams, Jonathan Davies and me in New York after completing the cycle ride from Boston. Hard, but fun, raising money for a good cause
Photo: Velindre Fundraising

Nice to get family and friends involved: (L–R) Peter Knight, Paul Guy, Georgi Hall, Charlie Hall, me and Andy Martin
Photo: Velindre Fundraising

vine, the whole stadium idea would have disappeared. He was very instrumental in some of the nitty-gritty stuff with the contractors as it went on, too. Club lawyer Alan Whitely spent hundreds of hours drafting the legal agreements and he brought a brilliant eye for detail which was necessary for a scheme of this size.

The people involved in this project at Cardiff council were very professional, but I think there were a few of them there who did their best to make it happen: chief executive Byron Davies, project manager Emyr Evans and head of legal Geoff Shimmel, they were fantastic. There were times when we would never have got it over the line without them leading us down the right paths on how to get it through. There were some quality people there, some big personalities who were good at their jobs. They were well aware of all their obligations to the audit commission, the scrutiny committee and so on. Sometimes councils let you down, but on this occasion they were magnificent – even though some of the meetings were necessarily tortuous.

When the stadium was opened there was a big ceremony with plenty of the great and the good in attendance for such a momentous occasion in the history of the club and the city. I was disappointed that more was not made of all the people who had played such a big role. They were invited, but pushed to the back. I wonder what they think when they hear Ridsdale on the radio talking about how he delivered the stadium. For any one person to take the credit for it is bonkers.

All those people played a part, along with many more, without them it could have fallen at any point. There was always an attitude that we could get it done, people working late at night, or early morning meetings, a lot of that went on just to get to the point where we went unconditional.

Without the stadium then the rest of the improvements in the crowd numbers and the team would not have happened, Cardiff City would not have reached the Premier League.

Without the asset of the stadium, would we have attracted the Malaysians? The answer is almost certainly, no.

Certainly Peter Ridsdale played his part. The council were understandably affected by the personalities involved. The irony is that when Sam Hammam went, Peter seemed a breath of fresh air. Suddenly there was credibility, which is maybe a little strange looking back now when Peter has been barred for seven and a half years from becoming a company director, partly on the back of his actions while at Cardiff and how he was paid.

I was on the remuneration committee of Cardiff City at the time, Peter assured me his wages were in line with the industry norm for a chief executive and chairman and I have no reason to disbelieve him. Where the money was paid into was within his control as chairman, rather than something that would affect the club, though the club assisted fully with the Insolvency Service investigation that followed. He is obviously serving his sentence while continuing to work in football below director level, but it was not something that affected Cardiff City and does not lessen the contribution he made.

On the positive side, Peter was brilliant in meetings, very good with the media and very plausible. After Hammam he was someone you could deal with. Peter was a businessman; he would sit in the meeting and listen, talk sensibly to people and understand what others wanted out of it. He was not a detail person, but he was sensible. He came with a tarnished reputation from Leeds but I think he took an unfair amount of the blame for what happened there. They built up £86 million of debt which saw them plummet down through the divisions after eating at the top table in European football reaching the semi-finals of the Champions League. They had a board of directors there but he was the fall guy, he was probably the most high profile but there were other people as well who were chasing the dream and building up huge debts to do so.

Peter had that reputation when he came to Cardiff, but he was trying to keep his new club alive. He did everything he could. He could not pay the tax bill, he could not pay the wages, so he was forward-selling TV income and doing deals with sports management to raise money against the value of the squad. Those were big problems for the club going forward, mortgaging the future to try and pay for today, but there was a pretty limited set of choices. One thing that did not change from his Leeds days, he was prepared to gamble tomorrow's earnings to support today – though he did it much more responsibly and on a smaller scale. He had a part to play in the Cardiff City stadium project, but there was a whole lot more going on.

When Peter arrived in 2005 the football club was in dire straits. Various directors stumped up some money to keep it going, Paul, Steve Borley, Michael Isaacs and I all put money in, there were many more who put in various sums. We all invested to put in the £6 million to get rid of Hammam and that money was only returned recently. All those people invested at a time when the stadium looked as though it would be happening and there could have been a possible upside on the shares, but I would argue they are worth now exactly what they paid. These are faithful Cardiff City fans who put in a bit of money to try and keep the club going, rank and file fans from all sorts of walks of life.

While Peter was there, Paul and I went back and fore to his office all the time as the cash flow problems were huge. One of the times Paul and I thought it was going to go bust, we went for lunch in Jamie Oliver's restaurant in Cardiff and decided we would be the only people to buy the club as we had first call on the debt. We would have been able to buy the club for a pound, so we decided Paul would have to go in and run it on the basis of trying to keep it going forward and searching for investment from somewhere else. He would have had to rationalise the costs being spent on players and everything else. We would have had to have taken the points deduction and probably gone down a division. Meanwhile I would have carried on running the property side of PMG. That was a scary conversation to have to think we had got ourselves into it that deeply.

To be fair, though, something always seemed to come along at Cardiff City to save things, whether it was an FA Cup run, selling Aaron Ramsey or Roger Johnson. However you always had the feeling with Peter there would be a last throw of the dice somewhere, that he would find a way out of the problems. He might have been mortgaging the future, he might have been selling shirt advertising cheap, but there would always be something going on. He took an incredibly positive approach to finding a way out of our problems and worked long hours to do it. They might not always have been the best decisions in the long term, but he did keep things going and I admire him for that.

To his eternal credit he did all that while there was a huge amount of pressure on him. Pressure from the media, from Dave Jones who wanted more players and money, trying to juggle cash-flows with the tax man, trying to keep the stadium project going, so he managed to keep the bandwagon going under all of that pressure. He had some huge slices of luck, too, like the FA Cup run.

If reaching the FA Cup final had played a huge part in 2008, then it was equally important when Dave Jones took us on a run to the Championship play-offs final in May 2010. To get that far and then fall at the hurdle against Blackpool was just gutting. The build up to that game was still the most nervous I have ever felt in any sporting event in my life. Never mind playing for the Lions or any of my rugby internationals with Wales, coming down that morning for breakfast before the play-off final was nerve-jangling. We knew we had a chance of going into the Premier League, it all hinged on one game and if we won it that would solve everything. We went in as favourites so to go 1–0 up and 2–1 up, thanks to goals by Joe Ledley and Michael Chopra, and then lose 2–3 as we did was absolutely gut-wrenching. You knew as well that after that game it would be the end of Peter, he had gambled everything and it had fallen. He was under a lot of stress at the time, so it would have been nice for him if it had worked out – but it was not to be. Thankfully three years later we reached the Premier League, but there were a lot of moments along the way when we did not think we were going to manage it.

The other question was wondering how fans were going to take to the stadium. We had a limited budget, but Laing O'Rourke and Steve Borley did such a good job of finishing it off on the budget that was available. There are a lot of people across the board looking to jump on the bandwagon now Cardiff City have been in the Premier League, but it is funny to look back and ask where those people were then. There were not too many of them putting their hands up then, especially when it came to writing any cheques.

PMG took a lot of the risk, we told the council we would take responsibility for any overspend on the stadium and we also fudged the issue of the fit-out of the stadium as much as we could to ensure it did not de-rail anything. If we had known what was going to happen to the economy in 2008 we would probably not have been able to do any of that.

One of the fascinating experiences of being involved with a football club, is the way it operates like no other business. Normal rules of business appear to go out the window. Wages and agents fees were at staggering levels, even in the Championship.

There are huge differences between football and rugby. You had a journeyman player in the Championship earning £5–7 grand a week and they might not play for a month because they were not being picked. When you earn that much to train two hours a day, it is a pretty comfortable living.

Then there was a later period in 2011 when Cardiff City's Malaysian owner Vincent Tan and Dave Jones signed loan players and tried to earn a place in the Premier League that way. I remember speaking to Dave when he had assembled the squad and he was very confident he had what he wanted to have a real go at promotion. Sadly, I think many of his high profile loan players let Dave Jones down when it came to the crunch.

They lost out to Reading in the play-off semi-finals. I felt some of those loan players did not show a long term commitment to the club and perhaps that was revealed towards the end of the season. Some of the players really ran for the cause of trying to get Cardiff City promoted, Craig Bellamy being the obvious example of someone who gave everything, while you did not see the same attitude from all the loan players. That cost Dave his job as he was sacked shortly after that defeat, with Malky Mackay being brought in to try a different approach.

When Dave Jones left it was probably the right time, though I do feel a little sorry for him that he was not given the money for players to build a side – he was always scratching round and penny-pinching to try and get players from here or there. I enjoyed Dave's company and for a long time he did a really good job with the resources he had. For example if Chopra was injured then he did not have another striker to turn to, as Malky Mackay and Ole Gunnar Solskjaer did.

Dave was doing it on a shoestring, which is why he felt a bit aggrieved when he was sacked. The purse strings had never been opened to build a side his way. He had built a side on loan signings, with some quality players like Craig Bellamy, Jay Bothroyd and Michael Chopra. Maybe there was a lack of discipline as well. He also fell out with the media, which is never a good thing to do, but I had a lot of time for him. We went to a couple of dinners and he was good fun away from that monosyllabic display in press conferences. He had a dry sense of humour and was well liked.

I really enjoyed seeing football from that close and comparing it with rugby, especially in terms of the attitude of some players. Malky went into enormous depths, with his backroom staff, in researching everything about a player. They wanted to know everything about the characters they signed. He ran iron discipline, simple things like no mobile phones at lunch, they all had to wear the same things after training, they met at the same times and ran to training. Simple discipline that you might think would happen automatically, but Dave had some difficult personalities to deal with. He had the likes of Chopra who had his well documented gambling issues, but there were a lot of mavericks there and on their day they would let him down. Bellamy was injured in the first leg of his last play-off season, which was a big loss, and the rest let him down spectacularly.

He did a very good job in difficult circumstances with the background that the club could go bust at any moment, the tax bills, the season ticket farce, so he was trying to work under that pressure with his hands tied behind his back. He had to gamble because he did not have the money to buy the pedigree of player he wanted so he had a team of misfits, if you like. There was a flaw in every player. One day I asked Dave about the inconsistency and Dave replied that was why the player was where he was. If he produced his top form all the time then he would be at a Premier League club, he would not be in Cardiff City. The ones who could sometimes do it and sometimes not were frustrating, but they were brilliant some days.

I think Malky is potentially an unbelievable manager, possibly a top four manager in the Premier League. He embraces knowledge from other sports, takes on board the lessons from sports science and he relates to everyone in the club. Malky had money to spend, but in my view he spent it wisely which is sometimes harder. Sitting behind the scenes of the transfers was fascinating. Cardiff was a selling club then, when Aaron Ramsey went to Arsenal for £5 million that was massive and kept us going, Roger Johnson going to Birmingham was also an important factor. Peter had those contacts in football and was able to do those deals to keep the club afloat.

I did find football supporters a little different from my background mixing with rugby fans. I got caught a few times after games. Rugby clubhouses were always pretty friendly, banter rather than anything more sinister, but in football there is always a certain element. I went into a pub in Cardiff after one game, around the time of the January transfer window, when there was a lot of speculation over Wales international and Cardiff product Joe Ledley being sold.

We had a good offer in from Stoke, around £6m, so when he went to Celtic on a free transfer a little later we missed out on an important payday. In hindsight we should have sold him to Stoke, but we didn't at that stage because I think Peter recognised the backlash we would have faced and we did not have enough time to replace him. There were a couple of boys in that Cardiff pub who had a few lagers in them, telling me that we had better not sell Ledley or else! There was a veiled threat there – it was a bit edgy. There is certainly a different element in football.

The fans marches against Peter were a bit unfair too, but he was remarkable – so thick-skinned he just took it all and nothing seemed to ruffle him when most people would have been upset about the chants. He was happy to walk into the lion's den of a supporters meeting and tell it as it was – warts and all.

There was a time after a bad run of results when Peter was wondering if we should let Dave go. He was talking to other managers and I think it was Paul and I who persuaded Peter we had to give Dave more time. It was mainly Peter's decision, but he did consult us. Dave took us to the FA Cup final and play-offs final after that, getting so close to the Premier League, so it worked out well as a decision. Dave was working under very difficult conditions from the time he joined under Sam Hammam, but it was sad the way it ended for him in acrimonious circumstances.

So Peter Ridsdale played an important role in the resurgence of Cardiff City and the route that has taken them to the Premier League, but he was one of many.

6

In the Red Corner

THE BILLIONAIRE MALAYSIAN owner of Cardiff City, Tan Sri Dato Seri Vincent Tan Chee Yioun (who has become known for obvious reasons as just Vincent Tan), is wealthy enough to give the club a chance in the super-rich world of the Premier League. Amazingly, the story of how he got involved started with a letter from a young Malaysian footballer asking for a trial.

He was the son of Dato Chan Tien Ghee (known as TG), who would go on to become chairman of the club and the key person involved in bringing in Tan. Cardiff were one of the only clubs who answered that letter and his son came over here for a trial. TG came over with him and Alan Whiteley saw an opportunity. Peter Ridsdale got involved as well and it was a time the club were looking for investors – weren't they always?

There were some Americans who were supposed to be interested in investing, but nothing ever came of that, and a Guernsey property developer Ben Steele who talked about a £40 million takeover. I took him out for dinner in Cardiff, we thought he was serious enough to arrange for him to have a private meeting with manager Dave Jones in our hospitality box at the stadium. One of the first things he told Dave at the time was that he didn't like our strikers and wanted to get rid of Michael Chopra, who was our star player at that stage. I thought the bloke was a buffoon. It showed how ridiculous the whole thing was, nothing ever came of it, but that was how desperate the club were.

We had football advisor Keith Harris in London helping us to find investors. We went on a wild goose chase to a Champions League game in Barcelona, with a private jet for Dave Jones, Peter Ridsdale, Paul Guy, Keith Harris and I. We stayed in a hotel there with the aim of meeting up with a Kazakhstani oligarch. I think he was there in the background somewhere but we did not even get to see him! It was just bizarre, but we were trying desperately to find someone who could put the money into the football club that it desperately needed to survive.

That trip may have turned out to be a wild goose chase, but I enjoyed watching a Champions League game in Barcelona. However I was amazed when I witnessed Peter Ridsdale getting abused on the way into the stadium by the Manchester United fans. He batted it off. I was always amazed with how he coped with critics and especially such vitriolic personal abuse. Our only real selling point for the debt-riddled club, that still had the Langston debt hanging over it, was the new stadium and the prospect of the Premier League.

TG joined the board in May 2009 and he became chairman in May 2010. He had a business partnership with Vincent Tan and was instrumental in encouraging him to get involved with Cardiff City. TG is a fantastic guy, it is really sad that he is not still involved. He was very quiet, hated any confrontation of any sort as I found out in one meeting when I slightly raised my voice on something. He pointed out, politely but firmly, that is not the way they do business in Malaysia. He is an absolute gentleman, the calm the club needed at that time. He was a complete contrast with what had gone before. He was a man of his word as well, took nothing out of the club at all – he even paid his own air fares and taxis, for instance.

You knew TG was not the main man though; the power behind the throne was always Vincent. We never got to the bottom of that relationship and we have not really found out what happened when TG left either. He just disappeared off the face of the earth, which was very sad for me. He put up with a lot of stress and pressure to help us get to where we were. He was going to come to our box for the last game when we went up to the Premier League, we would have welcomed him with open arms, but he pulled out. It was a shame for him not to be there that day.

TG did a lot to clean up the club and restore its image, though he did it very quietly. He built a really good infrastructure in the club along with us, with some good people connected to the area – at that time Gethin Jenkins moved from the Newport Gwent Dragons rugby to become the new chief executive, while there was also finance director Doug Lee who shared that identity with south Wales. That local connection has disappeared now the club is back to being run from Malaysia, by Malaysians and for Malaysians. It is their money so you cannot argue, but they got rid of good people. Call me old fashioned but I think it is vital for the soul and feel of a club to have local people involved, who believe passionately in what they are doing.

Vincent Tan came to the play-off final at Wembley against Blackpool and apparently it was his first game of football. I think he might have seen it as a bet – put £6 million in here and he might get £100 million for winning one game by reaching the riches of the Premier League. Sadly it did not come off, but what he has done since is nothing short of startling, amazing and long may it continue. What he is doing is every Cardiff City fan's dream. You cannot be a millionaire now in top level football, you need to be billionaire to support it. He is and I hope he gets them back to the Premier League and carries on enjoying it. I do not know how he is going to make any money out of it and he is already talking about an emotional dividend rather than a financial one.

I met Vincent for the first time two days before the play-off final. Paul and I went to the Cardiff City training ground and we saw a big bus driving in with a huge entourage of Malaysian press. There was a big 50-seater coach parked outside the training ground and Paul wondered how Vincent enjoyed the trip from the airport by bus. As we walked past the bus there was this huge Rolls Royce with a driver and it became obvious he hadn't come on the coach! He was pitch side, all the players were signing autographs and doing interviews with the Malaysian journalists, that was when you thought there was something big starting – just because there was such a huge level of interest in Malaysia.

The Malaysians have used Cardiff City quite wisely to bring people over who are Malaysian businessmen, investors, former kings, ministers, all sorts of people. Vincent Tan had bought a Premier League football club to market in Malaysia and the market out there is massive. I have travelled to Kuala Lumpur since Tan Sri invested. The taxi driver picks you up and they are either wearing a Man Utd top or a Liverpool top, which is why I understand his fixation with a red jersey. That is huge to them, it is considered a lucky and strong colour.

They have no real professional football of their own in Malaysia and they all watch the Premier League. There are all sorts of opportunities for Tan Sri in terms of marketing and TV rights. I imagine Sky would have been quite excited about having an 'in' to the Malaysian market as well so it works on all sorts of levels. If you look at the adverts round the Cardiff City Stadium now, well, I am pretty sure there is not a Kenny Rogers Roosters in Cardiff – they are all back in Malaysia and the stadium advertising is being done for the Malaysian market, it is interesting how it has changed and so quickly. I know that not every City supporter thinks it is a change for the better, but this is modern football.

It was also interesting being in the boardroom when the Malaysians invested and seeing the amount of money that was spent. The club was losing a million or two million a month, which appeared crazy, to chase the dream of getting into the Premier League. Many people will think the debts will have been wiped out by the amount of money available by reaching the Premier League, but you still have to invest, you still have to pay the wage bill that went through the roof with the quality of players brought in. Premier League clubs are big businesses.

I have only been in Vincent's company on three or four occasions. There was the board meeting where he revealed the plan for the team to wear red shirts at home games instead of the traditional blue. I also had a few conversations with him about Sam Hammam and how to solve the problem of the Langston issue. Vincent is extremely powerful in Malaysia. Paul and I travelled to see him, we were there for a week and saw him for about two hours in his boardroom. He came through a door at the back of his office boardroom, he has constant security and an entourage around him. I don't think people in Cardiff realise just how important he is in Malaysia with businesses that employ around 29,000 people around the world. He has interests in many sectors, including oil, gas, securities and property. I only know because I have been to Malaysia and seen first hand how powerful he is.

A man like that does not waste time, he uses private jets to travel the world. When we were having lunch with him in his office we asked if he would be coming to the next home game, but instead he was going to the wedding of a king or sultan. It is just a completely different world. It was intriguing to hear from his staff of how dedicated he is to his businesses and how hard he works. When they travel he is always the last man to sleep, always working, and a remarkable businessman. Paul Guy adds:

> He is extremely focused and successful. I do not know anybody else who would be prepared to commit £100 million, fund players, look at improving the stadium, improve the training facilities, buy out the minority shareholders, all with just one condition – that the team plays in red.
>
> To me that was a no-brainer, things move on. Without him you were looking at a very, very difficult time in the financial markets so the club could well have gone by now without him.
>
> He took a gamble on that play-off final against Blackpool. One of the Crystal Palace directors asked him how he got involved in football, he replied it was a bad decision in a moment of madness. He has moved on and got a lot more out of it now, but you have

to accept it is his team. That applies to all the Premier League owners, maybe that is the price of Premier League football. I wish him all the best in what he is trying to achieve. Maybe there are great business opportunities, but best of luck to him – he put out not far short of £70 million to get the club promoted. I do not think anybody else would have paid that price.

I know a few people will never accept us going red, but the vast majority would always back him. He can take the club forward.

I cannot see anyone over here getting close to Vincent. Former manager Malky Mackay seemed to have a good relationship for a while, but we are not sure how much Vincent understands football. Could he be another Abramovich and be a bit trigger happy with managers? I don't know, but it is his club and he can do what he wants.

I do not know if Vincent understands the importance of the fans culturally – and how tribal and steeped in tradition supporting a football club is. I was in the meeting when he talked about the £100 million investment if we changed the colour of the shirt. You have to have a certain amount of pragmatism here. If somebody says they will invest £100 million, effectively saving your football club, if you change the shirt to red, or otherwise they will pull out – there is not a lot of choice there really.

This red or blue colour for the home shirts is an issue which is hugely important to the fans, but in a business sense it is not as big a deal. When you take the colour of a shirt against the survival of a football club, does it really mean that much? £100 million to save the club, build training facilities, improve the stadium and get them to the Premier League. All that seems more important than the shirt colour to me. Sport these days is different to the old days, it is like a franchise, and it's professional in every area. You cannot compete unless you have a huge amount of money, so we need billionaires and these guys come with some baggage. Most of the teams in the Premier League are run by billionaires, it has changed the whole face of football and we are lucky Cardiff City has found somebody.

I don't believe the Malaysians have fundamentally changed the fabric of the club. It is still the same ground, same supporters, we have reached the Premier League and we can return. OK, they will not be playing at home in blue but that is a small price to pay. There is not a lot of money around in south Wales, so when someone like him comes along and is willing to invest you have got to embrace it – it is as simple as that.

When Dave Jones left as manager, I had a phone call from TG informing me that Alan Shearer is now our new manager, a real shock, but then he changed his mind overnight and in the end we appointed Malky Mackay.

It certainly made the promotion season exciting when we finally achieved promotion to the Premier League after so many near misses and so much heartache. I spent every Monday going onto the BBC website to look at all the permutations to see what we needed to do to go up – like 20,000 other fans, I suspect. The start of the season was pretty spectacular. We won five and drew one of the first eight games so we were challenging at the top of the table right from the beginning of the season, beating our expected promotion rivals Wolves, Leeds, Millwall and Blackpool. We thought this was a side that was beginning to motor. As the season progressed and we hit the top, you start looking at every game, studying the remaining fixtures and the point differences.

I was waiting for November, because under Dave Jones November had always been a horror month for us. I had my theory that the players were not fit enough when the grounds got heavier and you had to dig in. When we lost the first two games we thought that maybe it would happen again. But then we powered on through the rest of November with three wins and a draw.

At the start of February we beat Leeds away, following on from some good wins over Christmas. Having gone down to training and had a chat with Malky over a cup of tea, seen the players he bought such as Aron Gunnarson, Ben Turner and David Marshall, I developed a great confidence in Malky and the team. For example I thought Tom Heaton looked a better goalkeeper than Marshall, but Malky saw them every day and he was adamant Marshall was his number one. How right he was, Marshall was arguably our player of the season.

We were all so desperate to get to the Premier League; it was fantastic watching the run-in when we finally achieved that dream after being so close before. It is only human to wonder if we had thrown it away every time results did not go our way, but the strength of the management team and the fortitude of the players got us through. Wales international Craig Bellamy was brilliant, skipper Mark Hudson had a great season, Bo-Kyung Kim was good in midfield. At Christmas everyone said we needed a striker to get 5–10 goals for that final push – Malky went and got Fraizer Campbell who scored four goals in his first three games. Everything went right, to get to the Premier League was amazing and then to go on and win the Championship was great for the players and thoroughly deserved.

I had belief in Malky Mackay's managerial ability and still do, even though he has obviously been through some problems and controversy recently. When he was sacked the following season, as it turned out we needed 17 points from 18 games for safety in the Premier League. I think he would have done that, and then there would have been more money for players to improve the squad the next season and so on – he would have built something better year by year in the Premier League if he had been given the chance.

I thought Malky transformed the club, on the inside and outside. On the training field he brought renewed discipline and off the field he was excellent. From what I could see, he put in a new system in terms of scouting with Iain Moody. There was someone who spoke different languages, had contacts round Europe and they worked hard in identifying new players.

The fitness side, the sports science, all seemed very professionally run to me. It was a very happy camp and it was sad the breakdown of the relationship between Malky and Vincent Tan went as far is it did.

It started in the summer before a ball was kicked in the Premier League and I think it was partly because there was no strong chief executive or director of football to sit between them as a buffer. I witnessed Malky trying to do a transfer deal for one player by text, for many millions of pounds, and it seemed crazy to be trying to do business that way. There were different cultures and time-zones to contend with when any business on players was being done and I think this contributed to the breakdown of the relationship. It was a shame.

There were some great moments in the Premier League, in particular beating eventual champions Manchester City at home. It was one of the best sporting occasions I have ever attended. There was a sense of disbelief, and then to win at the end was fabulous.

I strongly believe if Malky had stayed as manager we would have stayed. There was some criticism of the way he set his teams up to be strong defensively. Well, he set his teams up to survive in the Premier League, to be hard to beat and to nick the points they needed. He was a strong man as a player and moulded the team in that image. I know he had targeted the last few games when we played all the teams around us at the bottom – and as it turned out that was when it unravelled instead.

I felt really sad for him it did not work out and he did not get the chance, at least, to finish that season in the Premier League and see where we had got to. If the two of them, Malky and Vincent, had found a way of working together then I think they would have been formidable. However that is football, everyone wants instant success and so many people get sacked prematurely. Obviously that relationship has changed spectacularly with all the developments since.

When Malky went it was a huge story across the world, it

was in *USA Today*, one of the biggest newspapers in America, would you believe. It transcended football for a while, it was strange seeing a Cardiff manager being cheered off the field by Liverpool supporters. There was a focus on some of the transfer dealings, but every manager makes some bad signings. He made a lot of good ones as well where the players have doubled and tripled in value, but no-one talks about them which I thought was a bit unfair. The squad he left Cardiff with was pretty good in my view.

It was such a far cry from what it could have been for so many reasons. When we were promoted the club was in the ascendancy and the owner should have been treated like a God for all he had done for the club. However there were so many own goals on the PR side, it was hard to believe. After being relegated you see the discontent now about the colour of the home shirt, but when we got promoted no-one was worried about the red shirts – apart from a small band of fans. You have to respect their opinions, but to me it was not a rally against the colour – it was a rally against Vincent Tan. It is showing him the power of the collective supporters.

If they do not bounce back into the Premier League then it will be interesting to see where it goes. Tan will have lost tens of millions of pounds, sadly, staggering amounts of money so he has to stay for the medium term at least. I feel sorry for him because he saved the club. Make no bones about it, Cardiff City were heading towards administration if no-one had taken over. We would have gone bust and been docked points. The fans would not have enjoyed that year in the Premier League, they would not have had the win over Manchester City or any of the other matches, without Tan's money. The perfect scenario for many football fans is for a money-man to come in, give the cash and then have no say over what happens. Give us tens of millions of pounds and leave the football boys alone to do what they do. That is very rare in any walk of life.

Would the fans prefer to be watching a team playing in blue in League Two? Some of them would, but I think the majority of the 20,000-plus watching them in the Premier League would rather have seen a team in red playing in the top flight.

Vincent Tan's arrival and getting into the Premier League was a dream that came true, but then went sour for some people. However the infrastructure is still there, the man with the money is still there, so if they make the right decisions going forward then there is no reason not to expect them to bounce back to the Premier League soon. Vincent Tan has to stay; his reputation is so linked to Cardiff City it is very hard to see him being able to do anything other than staying there without damaging that reputation. If you think about these very wealthy and high profile businessmen like Sheikh Mansour or Roman Abramovich, then no matter how much money and success they have they are basically known round the world as the owners of Manchester City and Chelsea because of the global reach of the Premier League. If you Google them, the first thing that comes up is the football club, so that makes it very hard to step away from such global publicity unless you can find a buyer.

Tan's areas of business stretches from property, oil, running franchises in Malaysia, lotteries, and much more, and he is successful at all of that. However Cardiff City is probably now his most high profile investment in many parts of the world and you cannot allow your most high profile investment to fail. They all want to win, Sheikh Mansour, the Glazers, Abramovich, they have deep pockets and Vincent Tan is in that company. He has the money, but the question is whether he has the expertise around him.

I think the fans will keep going to watch at the Cardiff City Stadium, but the team need to start winning again. I also think they could have more local involvement in running the club, through a chief executive, financial secretary or non-executive directors with roots in Wales. The connections between the club hierarchy and with the community in south Wales could be stronger.

It was such a far cry from when we first got involved. I

remember the last game at Ninian Park when we were beaten by Ipswich, a pretty ignominious exit from the stadium. Everyone had their hopes about the new stadium, but to actually deliver on it is a different thing. Stadia do not win football matches or championships, it is managers and money, but the stadium allowed investors to come in and see the potential. Vincent Tan and his advisors have seen the potential in this football club and stadium; they want to build it bigger – which was always the plan.

Personally I would not have expanded the stadium yet, I would have waited two or three years to establish the club at this level and obtain stability in the Premier League. Sometimes it is better to have a sell-out every week rather than the odd bigger crowd and empty seats on a regular basis.

The stadium, the development and the move has allowed the club to move forward, but I am under absolutely no illusion that it is Vincent Tan's money that got us into the Premier League. It will also be the establishment of the training ground at the Vale of Glamorgan resort that moves the club forward again. It is all going in the right direction.

We could have been at the bottom of the Championship for the next 10 years, but we have found somebody who wanted to come to Cardiff City and invest hundreds of millions. We should put the red carpet out from Cardiff airport every time Vincent Tan arrives, but not a blue one.

Part 2

7

The Packer Circus Enters the Ring

I ALMOST CRASHED the car when I heard the radio sports report on 18 August 1995. I was driving to a wedding in Monmouth when the reporter came on the radio explaining that a possible professional rugby circus, backed by the Packer TV organisation, would not get off the ground. My girlfriend at the time suggested it would be OK after a few beers that evening. But it would not be OK after a few beers. Not by a long way.

This was the end of a potential rugby revolution which had been building up speed in secret over the previous four months. The plan would have 'bought' Wales's top players to play in a brand new event. There were signed contracts being held in a safe at Eversheds lawyers in Cardiff that would have turned about 50 of Wales's top amateur players professional in a rugby equivalent of cricket's 'Packer Circus'. Those contracts would now never be activated.

That short report on the radio meant the death of a really exciting plan for the future of Rugby Union that involved almost every international player in Wales and most other top players worldwide. Australian TV mogul Kerry Packer had revolutionised cricket with his rebel 'circus' which had bought up many of the world's top players to play in his competition. It galvanised the game, improved the marketing and led to the players being paid much better wages – a rugby equivalent seemed long overdue.

The ultimate failure of this plan also meant that I was out of pocket to the tune of five to ten thousand pounds, money

I had spent and would have no hope of getting back. More importantly that report meant the guarantee of earning hundreds of thousands of pounds as a professional rugby player had gone up in smoke for the time being, for me and for many others.

Over the previous few months these plans had been secretly taking shape. There was a very effective news blackout at the time and it was not just the public who had no idea about them – it was all going on behind the backs of the Unions who governed the game. Apart from those involved, no-one knew the scale of what was happening, or how close it was to success. There has been an excellent book about rugby's Packer Circus, *The Rugby War* by former Australia lock Peter FitzSimons, focusing on the southern hemisphere, along with a few newspaper reports and autobiography reminiscences – but the full story of how it would have affected Welsh rugby has never been told.

It had all started with another battle between Australian media tycoons Kerry Packer and Rupert Murdoch. Murdoch had set up a new Rugby League Super League in Australia, taking many of the top players away from the traditional game which was shown on Packer's TV channels. Suddenly Packer, who had the reputation as Australia's richest man, was looking for a way to fight back. Rugby Union was suggested as a possible way forward, something that would become more attractive to him once Murdoch's Sky TV signed a 10-year deal with the southern hemisphere's main Unions in New Zealand, Australia and South Africa. Packer had bought out the top players from under the noses of cricket's governing bodies in the late 1970s, now it appeared he was going to do the same in Rugby Union.

The contracts in that Cardiff safe contained the signatures of every single top player in Wales apart from Lions wing Ieuan Evans. He was undoubtedly the biggest star in Welsh rugby at the time, but every other member of the international squad had signed a contract, along with enough other club or international fringe players to get two professional teams off the ground in Wales to play in a European Super League. Those contracts depended on the World Rugby Corporation (WRC) being able to get off the ground, but if they could put together the finance then we were committed to abandoning our traditional Welsh rugby clubs and joining up. It would have been like going to Rugby League in terms of the money and professionalism, but still being able to play Rugby Union for Wales. It was potentially the perfect solution.

We felt there were enough of us involved that the Welsh Rugby Union would have to accept it and run with the plans in place. We would be allowed to play for Wales in competitions such as the Five Nations, then, but there would be greater co-ordination between the southern and northern hemispheres as well. There might only be two Welsh teams, but we would be involved in thrilling new competitions around the world. We were excited – this was a chance for people who were international sportsmen to play professionally for the first time. I do not mean a bit of boot money, some appearance money syphoned through various channels to make it legitimate, but hundreds of thousands of pounds a year simply for playing rugby. Some of the guys were painters and decorators or carpet fitters – this was a big deal to all of us.

This was a time when there was a bit of 'boot money' at most clubs in Wales, but there was no big money in the game in Wales. A company called Alan Pascoe Associates had just approached 500 companies asking if they wanted to sponsor the Wales rugby shirt – but the jerseys remained without anyone's name on the front at that stage, none of the companies were interested.

And it was not just our futures as professional rugby players that might have benefitted. Would rugby in Wales be in a better place now if those plans had worked out? Absolutely, I believe it would. I really believe the WRC had a better structure for the global game in their plans than the one we have ended up with in the professional era.

Kerry Packer had bought many of the world's top cricketers

to form a rebel 'circus' from 1977–9. Many were banned for a while by their countries as a result, but the cricket was brash, exciting and high class. It dragged the world of traditional cricket into the modern marketing era. The players were far better paid than they had been and it paved the way for the higher wages of top cricketers now. Many of the things we take for granted, such as day/night matches and coloured clothing, were innovations brought in by the Packer Circus. They brought razzmatazz and excitement to cricket in both the way it was staged and the way it was covered on TV, it was an exciting prospect for professional Rugby Union to go down the same route. Packer himself was one step removed from the planning of the WRC, but he had given his backing and the aim was that his TV networks would fund and show the new events.

The plan for Wales and the northern hemisphere was pretty straightforward. Wales would have had two professional teams playing at the top level with big rewards – the Wales international squad would be pretty much divided between them with a few more fringe players to complete the two teams. Then the clubs underneath would have been much stronger, players who are now in regional squads would have been playing week in, week out for Pontypridd, Llanelli, Cardiff, Neath, and so on, it would have made the traditional fixtures of Welsh rugby far more meaningful, building towards the top end of regional and international rugby. The club game would have been a springboard into the professional game, it would have mattered.

The whole WRC plan was hatched in Australia, so I had first heard about the scheme four months earlier from Alec Evans, the Australian who was coaching Cardiff at the time and then went on to become the Wales coach for the 1995 Rugby World Cup. The reason I was asked to negotiate on behalf of the team was simply because I found myself captain of Wales before the World Cup in 1995.

That was a strange time as they changed Wales coaches and then captain weeks before the start of the World Cup in

South Africa. Looking back on it now, was it the best decision they made getting rid of coach Alan Davies, team manager Bob Norster and forwards coach Gareth Jenkins at that point? Who knows? We had won the championship in 1994, then we got the wooden spoon in '95 because we had a lot of injuries. Ieuan Evans had then led Wales more than anyone in history at that time, so maybe it wasn't the best idea to change the captaincy either. However a new coach often means a new captain and that's what happened in this case.

There was a political battle going on between WRU chairman Vernon Pugh and Alan Davies because Alan was pushing harder towards professionalism, which was right in hindsight. Alan wanted more resources, more time with the players and effectively to professionalise rugby in Wales. On reflection Alan was probably ahead of his time in his thinking. However Vernon was not just chairman of the WRU, but of the International Rugby Board as well, so there was that personal, political thing in the background. Vernon knew the forces which were going on, he was a very, very bright bloke, and he wanted to get control in his own back yard, never mind trying to control the world game. Alan, Bob and Gareth probably suffered because of that.

We have shot ourselves in the foot so often in Wales by getting rid of the coach and manager just before the World Cup. Alan and Bob were in that position themselves coming in for the 1991 World Cup when Ron Waldron resigned through illness a couple of months before it started. All the planning that Bob and Alan had done for the 1995 tournament in South Africa went completely out the window with the decision to sack them.

Just as with Ron, when they brought him in from Neath to coach Wales in 1990 and 1991, the theory is that you rely on one club that has been successful and try to transplant that success into the Welsh set-up. Cardiff under Alec Evans were successful at the time, so he was appointed as Wales coach. The theory of trying to base an international team round one club does not work. I know there was a huge amount of negativity from west Wales about me being appointed captain because of the rivalries and personalities involved. There was real rivalry, hatred almost, between the teams, which is what Welsh rugby thrives on. That was our strength and weakness in Wales, which Alan had managed to bring together to get players from Cardiff, Llanelli, Swansea, Pontypridd and so on to work as a team.

Ieuan was a popular captain and when I came in from Cardiff you can imagine the reaction, even though it was not my fault or my decision. I didn't covet the job, I didn't go to Alec and say I wanted to be Wales captain, I did not want Ieuan to be dropped as captain, it was just the way it happened. If somebody knocks on your door and asks if you want to be captain of Wales in the World Cup you do not say 'No', do you? The first thing I did was go to see Ieuan, who worked about 100 yards down the road from our offices in Cardiff, obviously he was devastated.

Then Alec brought a load of Cardiff players into the Wales squad. We had won the Welsh Swalec Cup in 1994 and the league in 1995, these were all the players he knew best and he knew had succeeded under his coaching. Out of a squad of 26 that went to the World Cup in South Africa, 11 of us were from Cardiff, just under half, including most of the fringe selections. There were only injury replacements then, so the squads were smaller than now. Alec was a brilliant, brilliant coach, the best I ever worked with, but in terms of being an overall strategist – well, he was thrown in at the deep end a few weeks before the World Cup so what was he going to do? He was going to rely on the players he trusted, which is why I found myself in that position as the new captain.

Never mind the pressure of being brought in as captain for the World Cup, I remember Alec ringing me about this Packer venture as well because a mate of his in Australia had told him what was going on. There were three key organisers of the new WRC, an Australian lawyer called Michael Hill, along with a former Australia prop and rugby administrator Ross Turnbull. The third was South African-born lawyer Geoff Levy who tended to stay in his Australian base.

Hill and Turnbull flew into Cardiff and I met them with Alec in the Holiday Inn, as it was then, on Mill Lane in Cardiff. I had to sign a confidentiality agreement before the meeting. We were supposed to speak to Kerry Packer's son in a telephone conference. It never quite came off for some reason, largely because of the time difference, and I was sat waiting there with Alec for a while waiting for that call.

All I really cared about at that stage was the World Cup and preparing for that, this was only five or six weeks beforehand and it was a bit of a distraction. We were getting down to the nuts and bolts of training hard in Wales squad sessions, Alec was trying to bring in a lot of new systems and it was not really working with all the players . There was a real reticence from some, especially the west Wales contingent, to working under Alec, which was a shame, really, and transferred into what happened to us in the World Cup itself. All that was my immediate priority, rather than some scheme for the future.

However when I heard the full ramifications of this plan and got to understand from Ross and Michael what a significant sea change it could be for rugby, I was excited by it. We were all under pressure at that time trying to juggle amateur international rugby with full-time jobs. In 1993, 1994 and 1995 there was an increase in training burdens with club and country even though we were still amateur.

I lost my job at Cooke and Arkwright surveyors in 1994 because I had decided to go on the summer tour with Wales, rather than staying behind and dealing with a specific project they had going for me. It was a full blown Wales tour to the South Seas, but looking back can I blame the partners of Cooke and Arkwright, people that I liked and respected? They had this bloke working for them, who they were paying, who had just disappeared for most of a couple of months during the Five Nations and was sneaking off many afternoons down to

Cardiff Arms Park to look at videos with Alec Evans, who was trying to do two jobs and probably falling short in the Cooke and Arkwright one. It was a natural parting of the ways, but those were the pressures players were under – and that applied to all the players trying to juggle work commitments and rugby during those amateur days.

When this WRC plan came up I recognised the opportunities, not just for me personally to be a professional rugby player – surely a dream for any player – but also the chance to be involved in putting the whole thing together. It is the dream of every sportsman and woman to play their sport professionally, partly for the reward and partly to see how good we could be – we were no different. To have the power and strength required for rugby you need to be able to train hard, it was very attractive for all sorts of reasons. It is strange to look back at how fiercely amateurism was protected, given that I believe professional rugby has improved the game enormously.

I was on a potential $200,000 contract for playing and $250,000 for signing all the players up. The exchange rate was approaching two dollars to one pound then, so it was an awful lot of money.

The interesting thing is that their model was to sign all the players and then ask the Unions to come on board at a point when they could hardly say no. WRC were going to give the Unions a 49% stake in the new project because they wanted to play in the international stadiums and share the marketing. This was meant to enhance and underpin the international game, not take players away from representing their countries – that was one of the attractions compared to the money in Rugby League.

They asked me if I could think of anyone in Wales who would be the franchisee for the Cardiff team. The obvious person was Peter Thomas as a former Cardiff rugby player and one of the most successful businessmen in Wales. I took it to Peter and, sitting in his office down in Cardiff Bay, Atlantic Wharf, I remember him immediately being enthused by the idea. He phoned a friend of his, Alan Meredith, a senior lawyer from Eversheds, to come over and they eventually acted on our behalf in holding all the contracts in 'Escrow' as an independent third party. Then, after the World Cup was finished, I went on a little roadshow around Wales to see the players and try to sign them up.

I went to Anthony Clements' house to see one group, booked hotel rooms to see others and various players came to my house. I managed to sign up all the top players in Wales at the time, bar one, they all signed conditional contracts and there was a date in September they were going to go unconditional, we would all get paid then and it was all going to go ahead in theory. The only person who did not sign was Ieuan. Whether he knew something that I didn't at the time, or just did not like the idea, I don't know.

After the World Cup, Ieuan and I were in Mauritius together with our girlfriends – I felt like staying there permanently after our World Cup exit! I kept talking to him about the Packer venture, but he just did not want anything to do with it and I respected his decision. He's a bright guy who knew his own mind, he was one of the few players who had an agent and was happy with what he was doing.

Ieuan was the superstar in Welsh rugby. We had started a company called Just Players at the end of 1993, run by Cardiff rugby club's former grounds man turned marketing fixer Albert Francis, through Alan Davies's Morgan Cole law firm. It was the front page lead of the *Western Mail* newspaper, as well as the lead item on BBC Wales and HTV news, when it was set up, seen at the time as a way of keeping Scott Gibbs in Rugby Union as he turned down a lucrative League deal around that time. The first players involved were Ieuan, Scott, Robert Jones, Anthony Clement and myself. Ieuan was far and away the top earner at the time.

It was headline news across the rugby world that we had got together to try to market ourselves, because rugby was still amateur, but the company could be paid for commercial appearances as long as we were not paid directly for playing. We could then be paid by the company, it was a very grey area in the ridiculous rules of amateurism. Unions wanted an amateur game, but they also wanted to keep the top players from going to Rugby League. You couldn't do both.

The issue was a massive problem in Welsh rugby at the time, with debates and TV programmes about whether the game should go professional. Looking back it seems silly now, when you have players going to France for hundreds of thousands of Euros. We had this internal fight, but is rugby any worse off for being professional? I think it is a much better game now, it makes me laugh to look back. There had been some money for players in Welsh rugby for years, so really the question was whether it should go honest.

The initial target for Just Players was a turnover of £100,000 a year with the bulk going to the five players, split up according to how many events, personal appearances, dinners and so on, we each did. It was approved by the WRU and fitted into the amateurism regulations of the time, bizarrely enough. We were dubbed the Famous Five in the papers, but the aim was to create a vehicle that could help other players as well. It did cause a bit of resentment from some, though. Of course it was just scratching the surface, we had seen on tour in New Zealand five years earlier how much further down the road towards professionalism they were then.

Wales was a very small part in all of this WRC deal. Australia, New Zealand and South Africa were the key teams they were after, it was when South Africa had just come out of apartheid and been welcomed back into international sport. That year's World Cup Final was between New Zealand and South Africa, Australia went into the event as defending champions. You could see why they were crucial to the success or otherwise of the WRC plans.

In the northern hemisphere it was England who were a big player, most of their players signed up and I was in contact with Rob Andrew and Brian Moore who were the main organisers.

Gavin and Scott Hastings were doing the recruiting in Scotland and Brendan Mullin in Ireland. I was in contact with all these boys over this period. We knew we were all signed up, but the southern hemisphere was the real powerbroker. The major stars of New Zealand, Australia and South Africa were heavily involved at that stage as well, there were contracts signed by the likes of their three captains Francois Pienaar, Sean Fitzpatrick and Phil Kearns being kept in safes in South Africa, New Zealand and Australia as well. It seemed a really great prospect to be a part of.

I put a lot of work in to sign the players, make the presentations and get the contracts signed. It cost me money because I was running around hiring rooms and all the payments were conditional on it getting off the ground. I spent £5–10,000 which was a lot of money to me. The incentive was so great, though, that nothing stopped me. I had an operation on an injured wrist after the World Cup and reacted badly against the anaesthetic. I was in a bad state, still out of it really, and could not drive myself so I got my girlfriend to drive me to one of the presentations – that shows how much it meant!

Money was not the only motivating factor though. It was something really exciting about a game we all knew had to change. It was changing already and we felt this could be something really fantastic. I am a sports fan and I had seen what Packer had done to cricket, so I thought this could be amazing for rugby in the northern hemisphere.

Some people may find this hard to believe, but I had massive pangs about only having two sides. What about the Llanellis and Pontypridds, all these famous clubs, but Ross Turnbull and Mike Hill were adamant there was only room for two franchises in Wales which had to be in Swansea and Cardiff, the major population centres and the major economic influences. They did not care about the history, they just looked at the numbers – what can you support rather than what are the historical and emotional ties about Valleys rugby and so on. They felt only two teams would be sustainable in Wales, playing in a European league and flying in and out to play. In hindsight, maybe they had a point.

It was exciting to be thinking that as a player you would be getting on a plane every Thursday and going to Toulouse, Dublin, Edinburgh or wherever. Of course they do it now in the Heineken Cup, but then it was all new. The Heineken Cup possibly came out of those plans.

I remember how excited some of the players were at being able to do this. These boys who wanted to have a crack at professional rugby, but had never had the chance, who were training in lunch hours and after work, trying to be as professional in their rugby as they could be whilst trying to hold down a job. It was extremely difficult and there was no career path, just the goodwill of employers. We had many famous players disappearing to Rugby League, there were huge pressures all the way, you had to rely on a kind employer who was prepared to support your rugby career and that was happening better in other parts of the rugby world. Professionalism was about wanting to become better players, fitter, stronger and more athletic. The players wanted the time to do that and it was the huge discrepancy between the southern and northern hemisphere at the time because they could put more effort into training, nutrition and so on. As it happens I retired from international rugby after the 1995 World Cup so I played in the last Test match when Wales players did not get paid – what sort of timing was that?

The World Cup was not a success for Wales, but I do not think this rumbling on in the background was anything to do with that. I went to one meeting about the WRC in South Africa, which was the day after we had been knocked out. All the boys went to Sun City for the day and thought I was staying back being funny because we had lost, but I was staying back for meetings with Ross, Mike and Alec Evans in the Sandton Sun hotel in Johannesburg – which was also where Vernon Pugh and all the IRB people were staying. That meeting was to give me my contract, getting me to sign a confidentiality agreement and then getting me to agree to sign all the players. Nobody was signed up at that stage, it all happened after the World Cup and had no effect on what went on out there, even if some players were aware of something happening behind the scenes.

There were other reasons why we did not do well in that World Cup in South Africa. Our biggest mistake was that we tried to play along the lines of what had been successful at Cardiff and all the players did not buy into it. Some of the players left out of the team let themselves down by going out drinking. Stories came out about that afterwards, so discipline fell as well and we tried to concentrate just on the team which was playing. You had two assistants in a coaching team which was put together at short notice. Mike Ruddock of Swansea and Dennis John from Pontypridd had both been successful at their clubs, but it was a combination chosen by the WRU rather than a coaching team singing from the same hymn book. I wonder if Alec was influenced by them on some selection decisions... there were two or three that possibly he would not have picked.

You also have to remember that we played Japan in the opening game and beat them well, then we played the All Blacks four days later. That was always going to be hard enough, but to make matters worse our team manager Geoff Evans stirred them up during the build up to the match. He woke me up one afternoon saying he had won the first battle because he had got the All Blacks sent off Ellis Park, the ground in Johannesburg, when they were doing their lineout spotting. I thought 'Oh my God, don't wind them up.' Then in a pre-match press conference he said we were bigger, stronger, fitter and faster than them – what a muppet! All Blacks skipper Sean Fitzpatrick asked me afterwards to thank our team manager for doing his team talk for him.

We did not play that badly in the game, we lost 34–9 but losing to that All Blacks side was no disgrace – they beat England 45–29 – and there were signs we were playing better.

They were a fantastic team, they had some great players such as Jonah Lomu and went on to reach the final, before being beaten by hosts South Africa in extra-time. They were ahead of their time in many ways, while Lomu was the game's biggest star, huge and quick on the wing. The problem was that we had to turn round and play Ireland four days later, we had three games in eight days and that All Blacks game took so much out of us – I remember being physically exhausted after the game.

This goes back to Alan Davies and Bob Norster being sacked just before the World Cup. They had realised, on the South Seas tour in particular, that you could not play three internationals in a week. You had to have almost two sides to be able to manage that schedule and pick the games you would play your first team. We did not make many changes going through that World Cup, a lot of players did not play at all. We played Saturday against Japan, which was a tough game we won 57–10. We played again on the Wednesday against the All Blacks and then had to front up for the biggest game of all against Ireland on the Sunday. Eleven of the 15 players that started against Ireland had started against New Zealand, we only used 21 players in total for the three games. Ireland had played New Zealand first, then Japan in midweek. They had rested nearly half their side, including half their forwards, for the Japan match, with eight days since they had played New Zealand.

I was still sore and tired warming up for the Ireland game and a lot of players were the same. I am not making excuses but playing New Zealand midweek and Ireland on a Sunday was asking a lot, if you asked players to do that now they would laugh at you. What Bob and Alan had realised was that we had to plan for it, they had mapped out how we were going to go through in terms of selection – and that all got thrown out with them.

Alec just picked the best players he thought would go out and do the job. Then he had problems with some players and the other coaches involved, so it all became a mish-mash. We

THE MIKE HALL STORY

fell badly behind early on to Ireland, but in the end we only lost by a point, 24–23. Even now I think it was a real shame because if we had won that game and then had another week together we would have put up a better fight against France in the quarter-finals in Durban than Ireland did, but it was not to be.

That match against Ireland was a terrible game, probably one of the worst World Cup contests ever. For example, one of the tactics we had was to kick the ball long to take advantage of the thinner air at altitude to get field position deep in the Ireland half. It did not work, the ball just went dead and they kicked it back from the 22 drop out so we ended up back where we started in our half.

We finished strongly in the last 20 minutes which was amazing really, but I think we were pretty fit. For a lot of reasons we came up short and we got hammered in the press and rightly so. We just had to say we were not good enough and front up. However if you think of it now, when a Wales team takes the field they are prepared in every possible way whereas we were a bit gung-ho, with all the work that had gone before with Alan and Bob being ripped up. New Zealand topped our group, predictably, Ireland were second and we were out in the group stages for the second World Cup running.

So that was the end of the World Cup for us, unfortunately, and the beginning of moving towards a new world for Rugby Union in Wales and the world. There were many meetings going on in South Africa, Australia and New Zealand and the Unions got wind of what was happening. The southern hemisphere's Unions in New Zealand, Australia and South Africa signed a big money deal with Rupert Murdoch's Sky and announced it during the tournament, but the players stood firmly behind the WRC for a couple of months after that.

I just concentrated on what I had to do in Wales, I did not concern myself with what was going on at a global level. I picked Ross Turnbull up from Cardiff Airport for one flying visit as he was running round the world trying to make the deal happen, but apart from that I did not know too much about what was going on elsewhere. In fact the southern hemisphere Unions had heard about the plans and were fighting back to try and keep the players with them, but we were not involved in that. I signed up around 50 players in Wales, enough for two teams here, but unfortunately things did not work out in the southern hemisphere where the real power struggle was.

During this period while I was getting the contracts signed post-World Cup, word reached Vernon Pugh what I was doing and he gave me a ring. It was literally a two-minute conversation where he said he had heard what I was doing. I had given up international rugby, I had nothing to lose then really, I had firmly nailed my colours to the mast with Ross and Michael to try and get this thing done. Vernon was a top bloke, and I just told him it was true, I would not lie to him, I was signing players. I held Vernon in huge respect, he was a top planning QC, a brilliant administrator and I really liked him.

I am sure Vernon knew what was going on anyway, so I told him everything that was happening. There was a huge amount going on in the press with the idea that the 1995 World Cup would be a watershed anyway – as it proved. After that I think Vernon just took a lead in the world game, the reason they unduly rushed in professionalism at the end of that August was that they knew of the threat from Packer – and others potentially – so they wanted the Unions to keep control of the game. Of course that created a different chaos. Vernon was the main boss and he was not going to let professionalism happen here in Wales first, there were no counter-offers to players to lure them away from the WRC as there were in the southern hemisphere.

But I was honest also because there was a feeling something was going to change – and we all wanted it to. It was an exciting time, going to all those meetings was quite something to be involved in. Alec was a key player because of the people he knew in Australia, I trusted Alec and so I went along with it.

A week after the collapse of the WRC, Vernon Pugh chaired

an International Rugby Board meeting in Paris on 26 August which decided to change the amateur game of Rugby Union for ever. It would now be an open game – or professional, to put it more simply. The Unions had lost the battle to keep it amateur, but won the battle to keep control of the game.

The outcome of becoming a professional in Cardiff was a bit of a joke because they thought being a professional meant training all the time, which was too much – we were constantly knackered. I was doing three days a week with our new company Steepholm, two days on the commercial side at Cardiff and playing as well – it was all smoke and mirrors. Whereas before I used to slip out of work in an office to go training, watch videos or make rugby plans, now I was slipping out of weights sessions to put a suit on and go to work. Our coach Terry Holmes soon worked out what was going on.

It was too late for me, I was 30 and could not give up work for a couple of years to give it a go so I combined the two – even though that was really difficult. It had all changed very sudden, though. The money was not as big as it would have been under the WRC, but it was still a dramatic change for Wales's rugby players. I went from earning a bit of boot money to suddenly earning £50–60,000 a year with Cardiff. I took on an extra role helping out as commercial manager at Cardiff RFC as well. Another part of the fall-out was suggesting to Peter Thomas that since the franchise had fallen through, why not buy Cardiff rugby club? That was how he got involved and he blames me to this day!

As for the World Rugby Corporation? Well I am sad it did not take off, it would have been amazing. Looking back now, I think we would definitely have been better off in Wales. Look at what Packer did to the sleepy game of cricket, it completely transformed it into what it is now. We would have benefitted from all the southern hemisphere marketing and style of television coverage, improved staging of games, and it would have made a massive difference.

Now in rugby the English league is exceptionally strong

but they still play each other all the time, they have not won the Heineken Cup for a while and sometimes they come outside and find they are not as good as they think they are. It is extraordinary to get 80,000 crowds at Twickenham and Wembley to watch a club game, but I think that is what we would have had in Wales under WRC. We would have crowds like that at the Millennium Stadium watching the equivalent of Super 14 or 15 rugby.

There would have been a switch to align with the southern hemisphere season as well so we would have been playing more summer rugby – a much better game for people to watch. There would also have been more scope for the best sides in the north and south to face each other, which would have been pretty exciting for players and fans alike.

I think a Cardiff franchise, with all the Wales stars playing out of the Millennium Stadium against Saracens, Toulouse, or whoever, would have really taken off. They had a blank sheet of paper, but all these years after professional rugby came to Wales we are still struggling to come to terms with it. It is still a mess, our four regions are struggling to finance themselves. You have someone like Peter Thomas who has been bankrolling Cardiff Blues for years with little prospect of getting his money back. I admire what Peter and the other owners have done for Welsh rugby, but they have been let down by in-fighting and the lack of a genuine plan.

The Blues flirted with going to the Cardiff City Stadium but had to go back. People just were not turning up and people are not turning up to see regional rugby. They will continue not to turn up because the product is not right. If it had been Cardiff against Swansea, or whatever those teams got called, playing against each other in a relegation game or for a place in the later stages or a semi-final of the European super league, those would have been massive games. Underneath that most of the squad players would have been back playing the Welsh club game at Sardis Road, the Gnoll, and so on. That would have been a much better competition which could have maintained the interest, those players would be trying to get up to the European and international level and there could have been three structured parts to the season to maintain and build on the historical rugby interest. The traditional Cardiff v Llanelli game, for example, would have had real meaning, many of the professional players would have been involved.

That sort of rivalry was the lifeblood of the game in Wales. We should have a thriving club game with a clear pathway to the top, if you had that then you would still have people supporting it. Instead a huge part of the Welsh rugby public have been turned off rugby because of the structures and the product on the pitch. At the moment it is unsustainable.

It is such a shame because we would have had a chance to really brand it, market it and push those two top professional teams. It would have been entirely professional, there could have been players coming in from other parts of the world, it would have been like the Super 14. I really think it would have worked, no question it would have captured the public's imagination as the Packer Circus in cricket did.

It was a real pity it did not happen, it would have been the best thing – and not just for me!

8

Cambridge v Wales?

BIZARRELY IT WAS not a difficult decision, even though 99.9% of people would not understand why I made the choice I did.

It is even stranger to think of now, but at the time it was pretty straightforward when I was given the choice between earning my fourth cap for Wales or playing in the 1988 Varsity Match at Twickenham for Cambridge University. I chose Cambridge without hesitation, even if it meant I was left out of the Wales international set-up for a while. No-one would believe it now, but then things were very different.

As it turned out I ended up playing both and it was a rubbish week when you look back on it. We lost the Varsity Match on Tuesday and then Wales lost to Romania on the Saturday. It was Jonathan Davies's last game for Wales before going to Rugby League too.

I got into the Wales B side in 1987 and also went up to Cambridge that year, playing for Bridgend occasionally. While finishing at Cardiff University I had offers from both Oxford and Cambridge but chose the latter because I knew the Land Economy degree was a good one to do. I knew some other people had done it before, Andy Martin, a friend of mine, and Gavin Hastings to name just two, so it was a well-trodden path. It set up my business career so it was a good decision.

When I got to Cambridge I was blown away by the place, probably a little intimidated. There are people who are privileged who go there, but there are a lot of who are not as well. The architecture and feel of it, everything is magnificent and the welcome into the rugby club made it even better. Tony

Rodgers was the main man there and he was a fantastic coach, the rugby was so well organised and we were so well looked after. You see all the names of the old Blues on the walls of the clubhouse at Grange Road to add to the history, from Mike Gibson to Gerald Davies, I completely fell in love with it.

In my first year Cambridge won the 1987 Varsity Match 15–10 against the odds, which was a great feeling. Oxford were captained by Wallaby Bill Calcraft and had two of his Australian colleagues in second row Bill Campbell and full back Rob Egerton, as well as All Black World Cup wining captain David Kirk and England prop Victor Ubogu. We had a pretty good side too, I played with England centre Fran Clough in midfield, England wing Chris Oti got two tries, up front we had the likes of Rob Wainwright who went on to captain Scotland.

At Cambridge everything was really well organised, the approach was very 'professional' for Rugby Union at that stage. Of course it was genuinely amateur in terms of payment, unlike Welsh rugby then, but we were fitter than the Welsh clubs as we trained every day. A lot of the Welsh teams came up to play us in Cambridge's Grange Road ground thinking they were going to have it easy against a bunch of students, but we blew everyone away. We had great coaches, facilities and players, so I really enjoyed the rugby at Cambridge and it did me a lot of good as a player.

A few weeks later I was selected for a place on the bench for the 1988 Five Nations game against England at Twickenham. That was my first introduction to international rugby which was quite an eye-opener. The invitation came in the form of the hand-written words 'England v Wales, 6 February 1988' on a WRU letter, all very formal and exciting.

Nowadays a Wales squad would be together for at least a week before an international, usually at least two weeks, training every day as well as doing fitness and the analysis on their opponents. Back then we did not get together until shortly before the game, usually the first training session was the Thursday before the game. If it was a home game in Cardiff then some of us would then go back to work the next day and we would not go into camp, so to speak, until the Friday evening. Away trips were slightly different as we would get together on the Thursday and travel to where we were playing, training there on the Friday. All the Five Nations games were played on a Saturday afternoon.

At the training session in St Helen's, Swansea, on the Thursday before the game, our coach Tony Gray stood on the halfway line smoking a cigarette watching the players getting on with practice. It was quite a contrast with Cambridge where things appeared more organised. At the Wales training session I remember them asking what we would do from a scrum in the middle of the field. Jonathan Davies said, 'all you lot go over there' – you lot was Mark Ring, Bleddyn Bowen, Tony Clement and Adrian Hadley, some real talent. The move was 'you lot go over there' and Jonathan would take channel one ball, quick possession from the scrum, and go the other way on his own.

I remember thinking what a rubbish move that was, with little thought or imagination. How wrong was I? If you watch the game Jonathan does it a couple of times to good effect, including skimming round England flanker Micky Skinner to start the move that led to left wing Adrian Hadley's match-winning second try. Maybe not such a rubbish move after all, then.

We won the game 11–3 with two tries for Adrian, our last win at Twickenham until 2008. It was a great win and a great performance with some typical Welsh flair, which sparked massive celebrations. From a personal point of view, those were the days when substitutes only came on for injuries and I did not get on which of course is disappointing and frustrating. I remember drinking on the bus from Twickenham on the way to the Hyde Park Hilton in the centre of London for the dinner that evening. You have been playing international rugby so the last thing you should be doing is drinking lots of lager and beer, but that is just what we did in those days. Everyone was dressed in their black ties and I remember some members of the WRU committee, old guys, coming down the steps of the hotel chucking a ball around up in the air. Someone said to Pontypool prop Staff Jones to go and tackle them, so he did. He ploughed straight into the old guys in the foyer of the hotel, scattering them everywhere. It was very amusing.

At the post-match dinner they put all the reserve players on one table, number 25 near the back. I've still got the match programme, signed by all the players, and the menu card. You had all the adrenaline of getting ready for an international and then the massive disappointment of not getting on – especially if you were like me and did not have a cap. There was one way you dealt with it at dinner; everyone got stuck into the free booze.

Glenn Webbe was sitting next to me, he was a clubmate at Bridgend and had been the first black player to represent Wales when he made his debut a couple of years earlier. Although he played on the wing, he had strength to go with his speed. At the dinner he had brought a laughter box with him, a gimmick from a joke shop. When the president of the RFU was speaking he opened up the laughter box and this raucous sound came out. England flanker Mickey Skinner looked over. He might have been shown up for pace in the game by Jonathan Davies, but he had a reputation as one of the hard men of the England pack – nicknamed 'Mick the Munch' because of his strong tackling. He came across from his table, wearing his Union Jack waistcoat, picked up the laughter box and put it straight into Webby's pint. I thought they were about to start a fight at the dinner, but the way they settled it was to go into one of the ante-rooms, both stripped to the waist and had an arm wrestling contest – an unbelievable sight. Webby won 3–0. I'm pretty sure that sort of thing does not happen in rugby now as they are so professional.

That year we won the Triple Crown with some great rugby and spectacular tries from the likes of Jonathan Davies and Ieuan Evans that are still replayed all the time, but I did not get on the field once so I did not get a cap. We had some really top class players, a backline of Robert Jones, Jonathan, Bleddyn Bowen, Mark Ring, Adrian Hadley, Ieuan and Paul Thorburn coming in for the injured Anthony Clement at full back. Welsh rugby was on a high, but at the end of that season we went to New Zealand on tour in the summer which is always an incredibly difficult proposition – it turned out to be a total disaster.

We went there as Five Nations champions and with a fantastic side, including such stars as second row Bob Norster, scrum half Robert Jones, outside half Jonathan Davies and so on. However playing in New Zealand is tough enough and we were not helped by the lack of organisation that had gone into the trip. The itinerary was brutal, Waikato first up, then Wellington, two tough games every week and then we had to front up against New Zealand. The weather was awful and people were dropping like flies, getting injured and flying home. We were sleeping in tracksuits to try to keep warm in rubbish little motels outside town, there were gaps under the doors with snow coming into the rooms on one particular occasion. On another occasion players could not get any hot water for showers or baths. Plenty of the heaters in the hotels did not work – it certainly was not five star treatment.

There was a lot of travelling, flying between games. You would arrive on the Monday, put on the local radio and it would be telling people to come down to Dunedin, or wherever it was, to see 'our boys' kick hell out of the Welsh on Tuesday. That was the highlight of their year and we were knackered from the game three days before and the travelling. Then it was another trip for the Saturday game. I ended up playing six of the seven matches. I scored a couple of tries and felt I did OK, but we got absolutely blown away in the Test matches, 52–3 and 54–9. The squad changed almost entirely during the trip. You would get up for breakfast and two more players had gone, flown home injured. It was a brutal, brutal trip. When we lost to North Auckland a bugler played The Last Post at half-time.

We would have struggled against such a great side in any circumstances, but the differences in the preparation of the two teams were a huge factor in the margin of defeat. Our build up for two difficult Test matches could hardly have been worse.

I got my first cap off the bench in the first Test in Christchurch, coming on in the centre. I went for an outside break against my All Blacks opposite number Joe Stanley and it felt like a car crash, I went back about 20 yards – welcome to international rugby. The rest of that game was a blur, it was so quick and they were so good. I started on the left wing for the Second Test in Auckland, marking John Kirwan – one of the all-time greats of All Blacks rugby. I still think the 1987/88 All Blacks were one of the best teams of all time. They had some magnificent players, even if you ask Kiwis now they would say that was a pretty special side – Grant Fox, the Whetton brothers, Sean Fitzpatrick, Kirwan, while Zinzan Brooke could not get in the side because Wayne Shelford was playing No 8.

We were so far behind physically and in terms of our preparation. Rugby Union was amateur, but not in New Zealand. The players were advertising tractors and all sorts on TV, they all had shadow jobs where they could train and play rugby almost full-time. That was the key for Jonathan Davies at the time. He wanted to talk to the Welsh Rugby Union about what he had seen in New Zealand, wanted to tell them we were falling further and further behind, but that was seen as arrogance by the WRU. It wasn't, he just wanted to get his message across, but of course they would not listen to him. We had a glimpse of what rugby would be like for the next ten years with the South Africans, New Zealanders and Australians taking it to a new level. In that crossover period between amateur and professional, they jumped across it much quicker than we did. All the northern hemisphere sides were getting blown away. Jonathan was spot on when he said at the end of that tour:

> A lot of lessons have been learned on this trip and it is clear that things must never be the same in Welsh rugby. The game over here is totally different, the way players are looked after, the way they can endorse products and the way they do not have to worry about work but can concentrate on their own training programmes, point the way forward for us. If we are expected to compete on the field we have to be given the same facilities off it. I am not sure if people understand that in Wales and that is why I want to give our side of the story.

The reaction in New Zealand was scathing, while the heavy defeats were front page news in Wales. The *South Wales Echo* splashed the thoughts of Lynn McConnell of the *Wellington Post* at the top of their front page: 'Welsh rugby's administrators need to pull their heads out of the sand. Welsh rugby is facing a disaster, these players are cannon-fodder.'

Instead the powers that be in Wales just changed the coach. It was like moving the deck chairs on the Titanic, Wales needed real, bold innovation but all they did was change the coach! John Ryan, who had been successful coaching Newport and Cardiff, took over from Tony Gray for the following season. John was the first national coach who had not played for Wales, but he came in with the reputation as a firm disciplinarian. It was considered that was what was needed to tackle the gulf in preparation opening up between the northern and southern hemispheres.

I knew at the start of that season, having been capped in New Zealand, the potential clash between the Varsity Match and Wales v Romania was on the radar. There was a seven day rule in Wales about not playing before internationals, I knew that and I had seen the fixture list. The Big Five selectors, as it was then, just assumed no-one would ever turn down the chance to play for their country so it was not a situation that was thought about or planned for. I had two caps from the

New Zealand tour, so I was not in a position to do anything other than keep my head down and hope the situation would resolve itself.

In those days the autumn internationals were not in one block of games, as they are now, you played occasional internationals against sides who toured one after the other. I played on the wing for Wales against Western Samoa in November, in front of a crowd of just 15,000. We won 28–6 but everyone was unhappy with the performance, we were expected to win by 50 points against the likes of Western Samoa. Maybe it was not as bad as it seemed, given that since then Samoa have beaten Wales four times in seven encounters, starting with the famous World Cup win in Cardiff three years later in 1991.

After that match the Romania game was four weeks later on 10 December. The Varsity Match was 6 December. I knew there was a possible problem, but just hoped that if I was picked for Wales then the selectors would understand and let me play both. Certainly I could not go in and make demands, but of course I wanted to play in both games.

At a training session at Waterton Cross police ground on the Thursday, nine days before the Romania international, the selectors came up and said they were going to pick me to play for Wales in that game but insisted I could not play in the Varsity Match as well. I thought that is just not going to happen. I went to the pay phone at the ground and rang the boys in my house back in Cambridge, Mark Hancock there was our scrum half and captain. They said they would back me in whatever I decided to do, but I replied that I wanted to play in the Varsity Match and that was that.

When you look at the uniqueness, the intensity of the build up to a Varsity Match, it was not that hard a decision. You would get to Cambridge at the start of the season, go on tour together and then there was such an intensity and camaraderie about the build up to a Varsity Match that it never crossed my mind I would not play in it – even to the extent that if I had had to make the sacrifice of a year in the wilderness with Wales, I was still always going to play in it.

Many people do not understand that, but we trained so hard together in the build-up, everything is geared towards getting to that one match without injury. We had played some great rugby that season, beating the likes of Cardiff, Bridgend and Northampton by large margins. I was the only full international in the Cambridge line-up that year, though there were a few like Scotland's Rob Wainwright and Wales's Adrian Davies, who went on to win caps. Oxford had three Australian internationals who had missed their country's tour to the UK over the previous weeks to be part of the Dark Blues Varsity Match build-up. No-one seemed to question that.

The traditions behind the match were very special. The week before the Varsity Match was full of special traditions. We went for a meal at Downing College, which was a bit like Hogwarts for anybody who has not seen a Cambridge college. The old Blues wore their blazers. After dinner we retired to a room with port and nuts, the port passed round to the left, the old Blues in the team along with some distinctive former Blues welcomed the new Blues. Then the toast was GDBO – God Damn Bloody Oxford. The team sheet went up on a board in town at the clothing shop Ryder and Amies opposite King's College, all the traditions were great fun, great to be a part of. Having done it once and won, there was no way you were going to give that up and miss out.

I thought the worst that could happen was that the Wales selectors might ostracise me for a while, but I could play for Wales again while I was only going to get this one more chance to play in a Varsity Match. Also I did not want to let my team mates down. I could not have imagined not playing in that game. It is really hard for people who have not experienced that to get their heads around it, but there we are.

The *Daily Telegraph* rugby correspondent John Mason

reported: 'Hall was placed in an intolerable position by an impertinent demand that he should abandon Cambridge in favour of his country.' That reflects the opinion at the time was not as clear cut as it would be now. I was quoted saying:

> I do appreciate the selectors' position and insistence I attend the Monday squad session is perfectly understandable – yet there is no way I could be away from Cambridge on the eve of the Varsity Match. I am so disappointed that I could not play in both games, but the Welsh selectors made it clear I had to choose. It was one of the most difficult decisions any player could be asked to make but my main commitment at the moment has to be to my friends and the University. I hope my chances of getting back into the Wales team are not affected, playing for my country is very important to me.

That still pretty much sums up my feelings.

We were favourites to win the Varsity Match that year, but we lost heavily 27–7. Oxford had a great back line, including an All Black World Cup winner in scrum half David Kirk and two Australians who would go on to win the 1991 World Cup in wing Ian Williams and full back Rob Egerton. My Cardiff and Wales colleague David Evans also played centre for the Dark Blues that day.

After the game, Rhys [RH] Williams, one of the Welsh selectors, came to the door of our Twickenham changing room and asked me to come training with Wales the next day on the Wednesday. I asked why as I thought I was not involved, but said of course I would go. Apparently there was a slight injury doubt over Jonathan Davies, but I was not told that.

After the intensity of the build-up to the Varsity Match, the feelings on either side after the match are incredibly different because of how much it means. It is the only match I have played in on that scale where the two teams do not sit down and have dinner together afterwards. There is a drinks reception together and then the teams go to separate rooms for the dinners because one side is completely off-the-Richter-Scale happy and the other is utterly crestfallen. The commiserations that night involved plenty of alcohol – I assumed I had no chance of being involved with Wales, so did not hold back.

I turned up at that Wales training session the next day and struggled a little after the night before. However Mark Ring was late as he mixed up the dates, thinking we would be training the following day on Thursday. He had a phone call in his office asking where he was and ended up arriving 95 minutes late. There were a lot of stories in the papers at the time linking him with a move to Rugby League, especially Wigan, so perhaps he was distracted by those overtures. I filled in at centre in the training session and the selectors put me into the side when they disciplined Mark by dropping him for being late. We were both in the shower with skipper Jonathan Davies as they called all the three of us out, one by one, to give us the news.

That week I had had the very intense build-up to the Varsity Match, went out drinking after the game and to top it off did not have a dinner jacket in Cardiff for the official post match function on the Saturday night after the Romania game. The WRU would not pay to hire one so instead I hired a car on the Friday and drove back to Cambridge to pick my suit up – anyone who has done that journey from Cardiff to Cambridge knows it is a long way – picked up my stuff and made my way back to the Wales team hotel before playing the next day. All in all it was not great preparation for an international, it would be funny to ask the boys now if they would spend six or seven hours in a car the day before an important game.

Then we lost 15–9 to Romania. I have never watched that game back on tape, it was such an awful feeling. I helped create our try for fellow centre John Devereux to score, but their pack were strong and outside half Gelu Ignat kicked well. They took us on up front and gave us a real battering. They had a strong kicking game, good lineout, just drove us all round the park. That was one of a number of games I played for Wales which were extremely disappointing, games we should have won. Once again though, I don't think we were properly prepared.

For example my preparation was bonkers really. That was not unusual, we used to meet for internationals on Friday evening at St Mellons hotel just outside Cardiff and they would allow you to use the golf course there in the day for free. It was a very rare chance for some of us to play on a proper golf course at a private members' club. Bridgend and Wales flanker David Bryant and I would usually play 18 holes of golf the day before the international, we were very naïve.

Then they would feed us steak and chips on the Friday night, we would go to the cinema and eat sweets and popcorn. Sometimes on the Saturday morning my legs would feel a little weary, there is no chance of that happening now with the sports science and nutrition, but it was incredibly amateurish then. We were still pumped up to play and do our best for our country, but we were not as well prepared to bring out the best in us and the coaching was naïve as well.

Significantly that defeat to Romania was Jonathan Davies's last game in a Welsh jersey before he went to Rugby League. Unfairly he took a lot of criticism for that defeat under his captaincy. At that time he was under a lot of pressure – he was the superstar of the Welsh game, he had been to New Zealand and had his eyes opened to what happened there. Of course all the money was in Rugby League. They came knocking at the right time, but I always think it was a terrible shame because if he had waited another year he would have captained the Lions in Australia in 1989.

The revolution against Communism happened in Romania in 1989. Their skipper against us, the back rower Floric Murariu, was a captain in the Army and was shot dead at a road block during that uprising. That was so devastatingly sad and puts everything else in perspective. It was just awful.

9

From Lions to Rebels

EVERY RUGBY PLAYER looks forward to the seasons when there is a Lions tour at the end, you dare to dream that you can play well and earn a place among the best players from Wales, England, Ireland and Scotland. Anyone who had been on a Lions trip will tell you how special they are in your rugby memories and in 1989 the Lions were going on their first ever full tour to Australia, who had emerged as one of the best teams in the world through the 1980s. It was the first Lions tour for six years, largely because of the continuing problems with the apartheid regime in South Africa. Traditionally the Lions had alternated between New Zealand and South Africa, but the combination of Australia's improvements and apartheid brought a change in 1989.

Unfortunately that year, Wales had a poor Six Nations. It started in Scotland where we were well beaten. I scored a try on the wing, but I only got two passes in the whole game and we lost 23–7. I got three or four passes as we lost 13–19 at home to Ireland. Following a bit of a campaign in the papers, especially the *Western Mail*, I was moved into the centre against France as we lost 31–12 in Paris. At that time Wales had never suffered a Five Nations whitewash, England were going for the Championship, so all in all we were up against it going into the final game against England in Cardiff.

The *Western Mail* headline on the morning of the game was, 'Our Last Stand'. The intro from sports editor John Billot read: 'Problems of deterioration in the ozone layer, inflation, poll tax and water privatisation all appear comparatively insignificant today when a more personal peril faces the Welsh Nation.' No pressure then, but the importance of the occasion certainly got through to the players.

Once we got to the Arms Park I have never heard an atmosphere like it, people really, really wanted us to beat England that day. The conditions were wet and dreadful, Bob Norster had a really good game in the lineout and Robert Jones controlled the match with his kicking. I scored a very 'iffy' try. It was a Rory Underwood mistake with a wild pass that missed Jon Webb at full back, the ball went loose over the line and I just got there before Wales flanker David Bryant and England centre Simon Halliday. I think I touched it down. If there had been a television match official watching the replay then possibly it would not have been given. Were hand, ball and ground all in contact at the same time? Possibly not, but it was all over in a blink. I always tell people to look in the record books when they give me stick. It was a memorable day to win, not great rugby or a spectacle but all that mattered was the win. The 'peril facing the Welsh Nation' was averted.

It was still a disappointing season and not many Wales players were picked on the Lions tour to Australia, there were seven in the original party while Tony Clement came out as an injury replacement. I was still at Cambridge combining doing my Finals exams with training and everything else. There were training camps before we went, which were good fun preparation for the tour.

In the modern game they have team-building companies to come in and get the players to work together on various exercises and challenges. Remember you have players from different countries who have to be quickly gelled into a team. In our day they introduced us and then locked us in a room with a free bar. It was different, everyone got absolutely slaughtered, but it worked just as well in terms of team-building.

The tactics of the coaches was to work us extremely hard in training and let us bond with a few beers at night. It worked. The spirit created in those training camps was excellent and it is something that has endured to this day. Recently we had a 25-year anniversary dinner at the Caledonian Club in London. There was a great turnout and the sense of friendship was as strong today as it was 25 years ago.

I arrived out in Australia a week late because of finishing my Finals exams. In those days that sort of thing was quite common on Lions tours, which were longer than the modern trips. I did my last exam in King's College, Cambridge and then got straight into a car to go to the airport and fly out to Melbourne. When I arrived the team manager Clive Rowlands was at the airport to pick me up. The first thing he said to me was to ask if I was going to go to South Africa after the Lions tour.

I was a bit dumbfounded and perplexed by that, I had been on a long flight and did not know what was going on. I was a bit behind the eight ball having not been there for the first week. It became apparent that the South Africans were negotiating with the Lions to try to get them to go straight to South Africa after the Australia trip. Of course it was the time of apartheid in South Africa, most sporting contacts had been cut off and it was almost impossible for South African teams to tour abroad because of the protests. They were desperate to maintain sporting links, had the money to encourage teams to go there and plenty of contacts in high places in the world of Rugby Union. No wonder they were so keen to get the Lions to travel there, following the cancellation of the traditional Lions tours such as 1974 and 1980. That idea fell down, I think, because the English were asking for too much money. They put the price too high, maybe deliberately.

I arrived in Australia jetlagged and went straight into one of the hardest training sessions I have ever had, in the mud and the rain in Melbourne. The first game I played was against Queensland. I was going all right, I got concussed but carried on. It was like playing with very strong glasses which aren't yours. I should have come off, but was so desperate to play I just carried on no matter how difficult. Everyone is rightly very concerned about concussion now, but players carried on more often than not then.

Then I was severely rucked, I had the shirt ripped off my back – I remember England centre Jeremy Guscott finding it highly amusing in the changing room afterwards. We won all the lead up games to the First Test and I scored a couple of tries against New South Wales B. I thought I had a chance of being picked on the wing in the Test team, but because of injuries to the likes of John Devereux and Scotland's Scott Hastings, while Guscott was overlooked for some reason, I got thrown into the centre with Ireland's Brendan Mullin – who had played against me for Oxford in the 1987 Varsity Match – for the First Test. I think we had two training sessions together before that game, alongside Scotland's Craig Chalmers at outside half.

We were well beaten by the Wallabies of Nick Farr-Jones, Michael Lynagh and David Campese, 30–12. We struggled up front and didn't click behind, they scored four tries to nil. Changes were made for the second Test with Guscott and Scott Hastings in the centre, England's Rob Andrew replacing Chalmers as the number 10, with English man-mountains Mike Teague and Wade Dooley coming into the pack for Scotland's Derek White and Wales's Bob Norster. The next two tests were close, but the Lions won them both to clinch the series with Ieuan Evans getting the match-winning try from a Campese loose pass in the third Test.

I played a lot of games on that tour, mainly on the wing, and scored a few tries, but only the one Test. It was a very successful Lions tour, one of the few, I enjoyed the whole experience and I really thought there would be another chance. In 1992 I had a groin injury which lingered for ages through to 1993 and affected my form. I was not in the original tour party for New Zealand and though I did get called up from standby, I could not go because I was having a groin operation. It was a nasty injury and took me a long time to get over that. By 1997 and the tour to a post-apartheid South Africa I had been retired from international rugby for two years, so was never likely to go. My biggest regret in rugby is that I thought there would be more Lions tours for me, another chance. It didn't happen, but I am grateful for the 1989 experience.

The idea of going straight to South Africa at the end of the 1989 tour may have fallen through, but then the offers came to go as part of a World XV, sanctioned by the International Rugby Board, generously sponsored by South African Breweries to celebrate the centenary of the South African Rugby Board.

My children question me now for going there in the apartheid era. I question myself. I am not proud I went. However I was a 23-year-old who had just left university with a hefty overdraft to pay off, starting a job at £7,500 a year, being offered significantly more for two weeks to play rugby in South Africa on what was an officially sanctioned tour. I am sure some players were paid more, some may have been paid less, for example some were paid less if they took wives or girlfriends for free. Of course Rugby Union was amateur so all rumours of payment were fiercely denied, though most people realised we were not going for the good of our health.

There was more to it than the money, though. I loved travelling and going round the world playing rugby, I accepted most of the offers that came my way to enjoy new experiences. However there was a huge furore about this World XV being put together with a lot of French and English players, while several Welsh players also ended up going. I remember persuading Robert Jones to go late on, Tony Clement and I finding a phone box in north Wales for him to ring the organiser. The whole thing was very cloak and dagger, we were not allowed to say anything. The previous year some French players had toured there, they travelled so secretly they did not even take any rugby kit in case it gave away who they were or what they were doing. In the end there were more Welsh players than any other nation, but only New Zealand were totally unrepresented among the major rugby nations. There were ten Welshmen, eight Frenchmen, six Australians, four Englishmen, one Scot and one Irishman.

The arrangements were all very hush-hush. We had a helicopter from Cardiff airport up to Heathrow and then flew out to South Africa first class. It had all been arranged by secret and we were trying to avoid the press at all costs because of the controversy. The aim was to get out of the country before anyone knew we were going. We were sneaking through the airport trying to travel incognito.

There was a feeling we were doing something that was wrong, but there was also a feeling we were getting well remunerated for it. There was a fear we could be banned afterwards, but it was a risk everybody took and the World XV tour had been officially sanctioned. My feeling was that if we did get banned then I would go to Rugby League. I got thrown out of my flat in Cardiff because I went. It was a very public event as well because ITV Wales were there knocking on my door to ask about the tour. My landlord at the time was anti-apartheid and did not like the idea of me going to South Africa, so he threw me out. I had to pack up all my stuff and move with the TV cameras waiting outside. It was not ideal.

When we were in South Africa some of us took the opportunity to explore the country. Four of us went to Soweto, Australians full back Greg Martin, who is now one of their main rugby pundits, and wing Ian Williams along with Bob Norster and I. We had a good look around and I remember being shocked at the scale of the poverty, I also remember being shocked by the other richer parts of Soweto with big houses. There are some very nice parts of Soweto, but of course the fundamental point was that the non-whites were forced to live there and categorised by the colour of their skin alone.

We visited a police compound in Soweto which had two razor wire fences outside and mines between the fences. We met the commandant of the police who thought we would be impressed, instead we were a little frightened, a bit shocked at how up front it all was. He told us how many people had died in

Soweto that weekend – a school teacher had been raped by one of the students, her family had been involved in reprisals and the police let the whole thing burn itself out rather than doing anything to stop it. Many had died in the violence. Ian Williams was asking some questions which were a bit uncomfortable for this guy, so he realised then we were not just taking in his side of the story. Ian was a trained lawyer who had also played for Oxford against me in a Varsity Match. He is now a partner in an international law firm in Australia, so the questioning was very intelligent.

The security around us on that tour was huge with armed guards everywhere. I was the only Welshman who played in the first 'Test' in Capetown, playing on the wing. We lost 20–19, so it was certainly a high class game of rugby. Then Bob played in the second 'Test' as well. That one was in Johannesburg and we lost 22–16, another close game.

It was great fun being part of the tour, because it was a great team. I will never forget the atmosphere at Newlands and Ellis Park. I played with the likes of Phillippe Sella, Denis Charvet and Pierre Berbizier of France. Sella was one of the greatest centres to have played the game with more than 100 caps, while Charvet had this dashing reputation, so there was some real talent and it was a unique experience to play outside such players. Those opportunities were a major incentive for going on the tour as well.

Before the first game in Capetown we went for a walk on the beach in the morning, Berbizier sat everyone down in the sand and gave this speech – mostly in French – but I remember being so up for the game and inspired about the great test of playing South Africa in Newlands as a result. He could inspire by the way he talked, even though I did not understand most of it! He went on to be coach of both France and Italy, you knew then he was a great rugby leader.

By going to South Africa in that era we had put the sporting and financial considerations ahead of the political ones. Did that matter as we were just sportsmen, after all? However by the end of it all I was getting very uncomfortable and insisted that I was picked up at the end of the second 'Test' and taken straight to the airport and out of there. I did not go to the dinner or anything else after the game, just got on the plane that night and left South Africa.

Was going on that tour the right thing to do? Probably not. Were we the only sportsmen to break the boycott? No, plenty went. Did it open my eyes to a few things about the horrors of apartheid? Yes.

When you are 23 and skint, money and excitement took over, though it came at a small cost. I got stripped of a couple of things – we were all on a United Nations blacklist for a while and I was also up for a sports award from Ogwr Borough Council which they took away. There was a lot of that stuff going on, but the payment for that tour was also a deposit on a house and paid off the student overdraft.

I like to think I know a lot more now than I did when I was 23. I would love to say that I should not have gone, but I do not come from a wealthy background – there was no safety net for me. I had been a student in Cardiff and Cambridge for the previous five years, so it was a lot of money to me then. I did not know very much about apartheid until I went and saw the scale of the poverty and wealth so close to each other. Apartheid is awful. If it was just the money then I would have gone to Rugby League, but there was also the attraction for a rugby player of going to play South Africa in their back yard alongside so many wonderful other players. If you can possibly take the politics out of such a thing, it was an incredible rugby experience.

I am sure everyone involved in running amateur Rugby Union then had suspicions we had been paid to go on the tour, but there was not that much of an appetite for banning more than half the Wales team from playing again.

Of course there was a huge row over the tour in Wales during and after the trip. It had all been so cloak and dagger, with a couple of members of the WRU committee involved in the process and famously a WRU photocopier and fax machine being used. That made it appear more official, but everything had been done behind the back of WRU Secretary David East, who was a former chief constable of South Wales Police. Clive Rowlands had become President of the WRU during the Lions tour to Australia and he also changed his mind about the South Africa World XV tour. He refused his invitation and the fact his son-in-law Robert Jones had gone was the subject of a lot of comment. It was a bit embarrassing for him. Clive resigned along with David East over the actions of some members of the WRU committee in facilitating the tour behind their backs, though he was later persuaded to go back to his position as President. David East did not return and was replaced by Denis Evans as Secretary, which would lead to its own problems for the WRU a couple of years later.

A special meeting of the Welsh rugby clubs decided not to have any further links with apartheid South Africa at club or international level. Of course the players were free agents, that was the other side of amateurism in that no-one had a hold over us. It was all very stormy and of course the players were involved in all of that, though as the tour had been officially sanctioned by the International Rugby Board the main rows were about the way it was done rather than the fact we went.

However one way of getting at the players was to follow up the rumours about payment. Of course the rumours were true, but admitting that then would have ended our Rugby Union careers. That was part of the full investigation into the whole affair by eminent barrister Vernon Pugh QC, which was the start of him becoming involved in rugby administration before he went on to be chairman of the WRU and IRB. It was also the start of a period of discontent in Welsh rugby that would eventually lead to the upheaval of most of the General Committee being voted out and a new breed coming in to run the game in Wales, including Pugh. It was very serious for a long time.

There were a lot of inaccuracies in the stories the players

were putting forward and Vernon was very, very bright, a brilliant QC. I avoided going for as long as I could because I knew it would be difficult. In the end they threatened me with not playing for Wales unless I went. It was a difficult hour or so, but of course I denied everything. They knew we were paid but brushed it under the carpet. WRU officials went on the trip enjoying the hospitality as well. We were not banned as a result, so in the end nothing happened to us. The players were pawns in the political game, England did not make as much of a fuss about the players who went, the French did not care, nor did the southern hemisphere countries, but we tore ourselves apart in Wales. Typical.

10

In the Shadow of the Threat from Rugby League

THE DAY A Rugby League agent walked into the inner sanctum of a Wales changing room to talk to me, summed up the threat they posed to Rugby Union in Wales. It may have been at the Brewery Field, where Wales had played a warm-up game against Bridgend, rather than the National Stadium at the Arms Park, but it was still a Wales dressing room and the scout just walked straight in for a chat at the end of the game. It was a surreal experience all round.

It happened in 1989 when John Ryan was coach of Wales, we played Newbridge and Bridgend as warm-up matches to prepare to face the touring All Blacks – we won in Newbridge but then lost to my club Bridgend. When you think about it now that was totally ridiculous and putting yourselves up to be shot down by the club sides, it was always a potential banana skin. The club players were really up for proving their point against the current internationals, who in turn were on a hiding to nothing.

The Brewery Field has a long corridor past the doors of the changing rooms, leading into the bar. It is a narrow area and it was always busy on match days. A Wales changing room is normally pretty private with people on the door to stop anyone getting in who is not meant to, but in Bridgend there were a lot of people milling about and this scout just walked through, came in, spoke to me and gave me his card. He asked if I wanted to get in touch, which I did later on. At the time I did not think it unusual, though it seems a bit mad now. I was always a bit wary of these agents, because the agent creates the business by telling you a club is interested and then approaches the club and tells them a Welsh international is interested in them. However in this case he was representing Castleford and their coach Darryl van der Velde was genuinely interested. I did speak to them, but was not really convinced it was for me so I did not pursue it.

It was one of those things that happened as you were going through the ups and downs of Welsh rugby, which was pretty tough at times. There were a lot of approaches from Rugby League and you were just keeping your options open. A lot of boys were going north at the time and it was always on your radar, never out of your mind, and players were disappearing regularly.

I remember this specifically with Jonathan Davies, having toured New Zealand with him, been in Welsh squad sessions with him and then played Western Samoa and Romania together. From seeing a lot of him, after he went to Widnes in Rugby League I did not see him for about a year. It was as though he had been kidnapped. You saw him on *News at Ten*, walking about being followed by a huge number of camera crews. I saw him the next summer at an event at the Celtic Manor golf resort near Newport, where the Ryder Cup was held in 2010, and he had moved onto another level in terms of his celebrity. Some of the players you mixed with regularly would go north and suddenly you would not see them for years, they were just snatched away. Any connections with Rugby League were frowned on that much, so it was a strange time.

In some ways that was understandable because if there was one big reason for the crisis in Welsh rugby with a few years of poor results, it was the threat from Rugby League. We lost a team, pretty much. It started with the likes of Jonathan

Griffiths, Jonathan Davies, Paul Moriarty, Richard Webster, Rowland Phillips, Dai Young – it was a long list. I always look back thinking that if they had all stayed, the likes of Scott Gibbs, John Devereux and Allan Bateman in my position, then I would not have got as many caps. However I would have preferred to have had fewer caps, but played in a better and more successful Wales team. We lost so much talent, it was a real shame and a disaster for Welsh rugby.

Jonathan, who was a superstar in Wales and went on to be a superstar in Rugby League, was lost because the WRU were pretty arrogant. He had to look after his family and his livelihood and it was big money that he was being offered, he had no real career or trade to fall back on at the time so for him it was a no-brainer – he had to 'go north' and join professional Rugby League playing in the north of England.

I almost went in 1989 as well. It was a different approach, this time direct from St Helens through former Wales scrum half Jonathan Griffiths and coach Alex Murphy. Jonathan Griffiths, who was at St Helens at the time, picked me up after a game for Bridgend away against London Welsh. We went up to St Helens, they put us up in a hotel, gave us some cash for a meal and some drinks and we had a great night. Naively I went into the meeting with the St Helens board the next day on my own, with no agent or representative, to negotiate a contract that was a £50,000 signing on fee with £25–30,000 a year. It was described in the papers as a £250,000 deal, which it might have been in the end, with bonuses, once everything was put together. To put that into context, at the time I was earning £7,500 as a trainee chartered surveyor with Cooke and Arkwright. Clearly the financial temptation was pretty strong.

The strange thing was Alex Murphy taking me outside and saying he could help me get me more money, because I was unrepresented. There were all sorts of dealings going on. We went out for dinner that evening and Alex Murphy was there. My girlfriend at the time was a solicitor, having been through three years of university, a year at law school and just got herself a job in Cardiff at a very good law firm. She asked about wanting to relocate and work up there and he looked at her with a bit of an old fashioned northern attitude of wondering why a woman would want to work. They had a bit of a falling out over it. He followed me to the toilet and said, 'Eh lad, it's you we're signing, not the missus!'

Little things like that put me off the whole situation. He also threw me a rulebook on Rugby League. I was supposed to be signing on the Wednesday in Chester and he was going to throw me straight into the team to play the following week. It was all a bit rushed and very sudden. For example when Jonathan Davies went north he was introduced to the game gradually, training at first, then as a replacement on the wing and gradually becoming a central player as he got used to a different type of rugby. It was mentioned in the programme for the St Helens game that day there was a Welsh international watching who was going to sign for them.

If it had been someone who was a little different, a little bit more sympathetic, more like Dougie Laughton at Widnes when Jonathan went there, rather than Alex Murphy who was going to throw me straight in, then I might have made a different decision. The team was under pressure at St Helens, he was under pressure as coach and it all spooked me a little bit. While I was thinking about it there was a back page of the *Independent* newspaper that said I would be the first Cambridge Blue to go north. There was a lot of stuff in the papers, 'sources' in St Helens were saying I had played my last game of Rugby Union. That all made me think too and brought home to me the enormity of the decision I was making.

Having just finished two degrees, five years in University, got myself onto a career path with a very good Cardiff firm Cooke and Arkwright to qualify as a surveyor, I would have been giving up on that career for the short term benefit of

Rugby League. There was a lot to consider and weigh up.

Looking back now, do I regret it from a rugby point of view? Probably, yes. I would have liked to have tested myself in Rugby League. When you meet up now with the boys who went, there is always an element of feeling that they tested themselves in that hard world and I didn't. However in my head I had a career mapped out, which thankfully has proved right. But I would have liked to have played the game of Rugby League, there is no question about that.

Giving up playing for Wales was also a major factor against going, I was in the team and enjoying playing international rugby even if we were not a great side at the time. It was a mixture of everything that meant I turned the offer down. There were other opportunities after that, but that was the closest I came to going.

It was a huge decision for people like Jonathan Davies, John Devereux and all those boys who did go north, but I think they did it for the right reasons to secure the future of their families. The people I blame were the administrators of the WRU at the time for putting their heads in the sands and not taking on the threat. They did in other countries, certainly in New Zealand, Australia and South Africa, while England were doing it in a different way. A lot of the boys in other countries were well looked after with employers who were sympathetic to the demands of international rugby. We stuck our heads in the sand in Wales and left a lot of talented rugby players to their own devices when they were trying to train, work and play. People in charge here did not allow for the pressures we all had of trying to earn a living while also being the best rugby players we could be. Some of those administrators had played at the top level, but in a different era when things were very different and their opponents were in the same position. Some had never played at the top level and did not understand. The rugby world was moving on, but things were slow to change in Wales.

Maybe it was losing so many players all the time that

affected our confidence at the highest level, it did not have the chance to grow. For example take someone like Allan Bateman, whom I first played with at Maesteg. He was a brilliant player, got his chance with Neath and showed how good he was. He did not have many Wales caps when he went north, became a superstar in Rugby League and then came back to Union when it went professional and was a brilliant player again for Northampton, Wales and the Lions. He was one of the best players I have ever seen, losing people like that at the peak of his career really hit Wales hard. You always felt you were battling against the WRU, they were so arrogant and sat back. 'We are the Welsh Rugby Union, this is how it has been done for decades and we are not going to change it.'

Rather than concentrating on how to keep the best players in Wales, there was a huge pressure put on the shoulders of the Wales coach. Every coach who came in was meant to be the panacea who sorts all the problems out, but it was very difficult for all of them – Tony Gray, John Ryan, Ron Waldron, Alan Davies and Alec Evans in my time. All the coaches had their hands tied behind their backs because of the structures, lack of direction and fitness training. There was such a disparity between say Neath, who were superfit in one way because they could run and run, while at the other end of the scale you had someone like Pontypool who were really strong and probably in the weights room all the time. In the middle you had a huge swathe of Welsh rugby who did not really have any direction.

Bridgend coach Brian Nicholas was very good, he got me to go to Maesteg when he was coaching there and then I followed him down to Bridgend as well when I had the alternative offer to go to Neath. He was a big influence on my career and stayed in touch throughout. He wrote me a lot of nice notes to encourage me through my career. He was very much a mentor and someone I respected enormously.

A lot of the coaches of that era lost their way. They were

coming into organisations which were too bedevilled with problems. The club game was too comfortable and too easy, there was no direction under the old Western Mail Merit Table before leagues were brought in. There was no real direction in Welsh rugby generally.

If rugby at club level in Wales was somewhat haphazard, then playing for Wales was not just amateur – it was amateurish. I don't think it changed for many, many years. We were on the cusp of starting to wake up as a team to nutrition, training and lifestyle, but we were way behind the curve. Cambridge were more professional than Wales, there is no question about that. Coming back to Wales was almost a disappointment because Cambridge were so well organised in comparison. They brought Phil Keith-Roach in to coach the scrums, Cambridge and England wing Mark Bailey was doing some coaching of the backs there as well. Stuart Storey, the athlete and broadcaster who coached the likes of shot-putter Geoff Capes, did fitness training with us. It was a great coaching team and they were not afraid to add other specialists when appropriate.

Every day included brutal fitness training. We had to do these runs round Cambridge called the Doc Turner, after Dr Mike Turner who was the Great Britain Olympics manager in the 1980 Moscow Olympics. It involved at least 60-minute runs sprinting, jogging, striding around Cambridge parks – which I hated, it was really hard. England wing Chris Oti and I were always at the back. We used to argue we were sprinters rather than endurance athletes! Our fitness was so much better in Cambridge than Welsh rugby at the time but you could not take advantage of that fitness when you came back to Welsh rugby because the game was so static and so slow.

The Cambridge game was about keeping the ball alive and running but Pontypool, for instance, were basically a pack and Dai Bishop. It was turgid, the structures were not right, there were no competitive leagues. Playing on the wing for

Pontypool – or even for Wales sometimes – was completely different to playing on the wing now when they get so involved. I got two passes playing in Scotland in an international, but that would not happen in the modern game – they get the ball in their hands much more so it must be a more enjoyable game to play.

It took Wales an awfully long time to catch up, I do not think it was until Alan Davies got involved in 1991 that these things were on the radar and it took a long time to change views on fitness, alcohol consumption, diet, and preparation for games.

After Tony Gray and John Ryan, Ron Waldron came in as Wales coach because he had been so successful at Neath. He based his approach round the Neath players who had become probably the most feared and successful side in Wales. I do not blame him, he trusted them and Neath were much fitter as a side than anyone else. He brought a fitness guy called Alan Roper in with him who was a runner, so we would have do six laps before every warm up – it was purgatory. We would even have to do that on the Friday before matches. What use was that, it just knackered you out.

I hated long distance running and felt I needed a more explosive fitness in my position – more speed training than long distance. He took us to Neath and we had to do some famous run there that they always did as a club. I veered off left and jumped through some gardens, finding a short cut and coming in about fifth or sixth. Ron thought it was great that I should finish so high and show I was that fit! Little did he know.

Neath and Llanelli hated each other and that came to the fore in the 1991 summer tour to Australia, which was an absolute disaster. It would take something to have a tour which was worse than New Zealand in 1988, but we managed it with that trip to Australia. Even the preparation for that was bad. I had a series of hamstring injuries after the 1990 match against Ireland and had not been part of the Wales set-up, but I was fit again and was recalled. Mark Ring was left out of the tour party, I don't think he and Ron Waldron saw eye to eye.

We were based in Perth in Western Australia at the start of the tour at a holiday camp which was damp and horrible. We were running to training every day on the roads, then running home after training. It was all wrong, there was no concentration on skills or tactics or anything. It was all based on trying to overrun people and you cannot do that at international level. To make matters worse, Australia had added Tim Horan and Jason Little in midfield to the talents of Farr-Jones, Lynagh and Campese and were taking the game to a new level.

There were good elements in that Wales squad. I enjoyed playing for Ron Waldron, I really did, after all I had been tempted to join Neath a few years before, but there was another side to the Welsh All Blacks. The changing rooms before the games were just a mad place to be with all the Neath contingent, it was a very strange place. They brought everything that had made Neath successful, just as Alec Evans would later try to bring everything from Cardiff into the Wales dressing room.

It was still a bit of a shock for a lot of the other players to see how the Neath players would prepare. There was a sense of violence in the changing room before matches. Ron put everyone in groups in the four corners of the changing room and then we would run across with balls, slamming into each other, pads and everything else.

I am all for, especially forwards, getting ready for the battle, the intensity of the contact, the hit and – if necessary – the violence. However there was no concentration on calm tactics, getting messages across as Alan Davies or Alec would. It was just a question of building yourself into a ball of fury to go onto the pitch. That is fine, but it lasts about five to ten minutes after the game kicks off. Then you need something more than that. I do think the Neath model was based on

100% fitness, along with some very good rugby players –
Jonathan Davies was the obvious one, but also the likes of
Allan Bateman and Paul Thorburn. Of course you had to add
the Neath pack to that, they had so many truly hard players
up front. They had a different mentality about them, but it
worked for Neath in those days at club level. At international
level you do need something different. It was never going to
work – and sadly it didn't.

We lost 71–8 to New South Wales and then the following
week lost 63–6 to Australia. We were completely outplayed,
they scored 12 tries, Lynagh missed eight out of 15 kicks at
goal so the score could have been above 80. It was still a
record defeat, eclipsing the results in New Zealand three
years earlier which had been bad enough. We were not up
to it, it was a very, very sad day and all the frustration from
the game was fuelled by a few beers in the evening at the
traditional function between the teams and officials which
follows an international.

Right from the start there was a horrible feeling about the
dinner that evening, the Australians were totally perplexed.
One Queensland official was quoted at the time saying: 'The
behaviour of some Welsh players had been bad through the
dinner with bread rolls and food being hurled. We have never
witnessed such a disgraceful scene at Ballymore and never
want to again.'

After the dinner – and a few more beers – the Neath
and Llanelli boys were arguing with each other and it got
very heated. I got to it late but found myself in the middle
– actually trying to be a peacemaker, would you believe. I
am not sure now what caused the argument, either style of
play or talking to the press, or a mixture of the two, but it
was very agitated on both sides. I ended up getting glassed in
the wrist by Neath and Wales second row Gareth Llewellyn,
it was an almost accidental thing that came out of trying to
keep the Neath and Llanelli contingents apart.

Of course that made headlines around the rugby world. I

needed three stitches and have still got the scar on my wrist. It was a nasty cut with blood everywhere and I had to be taken downstairs in the ground to be stitched up by WRU doctor Malcolm Downes. Ieuan Evans came with me and we ended up in a nightclub in Brisbane with my hand stitched up!

It was a massive story, both in Wales and Australia. It was an awful time for me and Welsh rugby. Flying back to Heathrow there were a lot of press, people were doorstepping me there and back in Wales. I did have feelings at the time that I had had enough of playing for Wales and I was tempted to throw it all in. I was not alone in thinking that. The papers reported that three other players would not play under Ron Waldron again, while three more were considering their position. Needless to say they were all from clubs other than Neath.

Wales were branded 'a disgrace to world rugby' on the front page of the *South Wales Echo*. It showed the state we had reached on and off the field. Cartoonist Gren summed it up on that same front page of the *Echo* with two Wales players walking off the pitch, one saying to the other: 'At least my Mum's proud of me. I don't tell her I play for Wales, she thinks I'm a bouncer at a strip club!'

I don't blame Neath, but there was always that undercurrent when you went to the Gnoll. Cardiff travelled in a blazer and tie, they had no time for any dress code at the Gnoll and they revelled in the fact they were farmers and hard as nails. That was the way they played, they were good, very good, with some pretty tough customers there as well. They were hugely disciplined on the pitch but there was a feeling off the pitch that they could do what they wanted. Former Cambridge, Neath and Wales second row Brian Thomas was in charge there, a very intimidating man. He was a very generous man as well, I know he helped me get to Cambridge for example. That undercurrent of the Neath mentality came through in the Wales squad a bit and it caused divisions during that period.

That to me sums up the Welsh mentality, the best of us and the worst of us. We can tear each other apart in sport and in business, but if we are moving in the same direction then we can be really formidable. I have witnessed it in all sorts of different areas. However sometimes in Wales we are very good at dragging ourselves down and we did that with Wales under Ron. He was ill after that trip, he got very stressed out with the whole situation.

It meant that just a few months before the 1991 World Cup, Wales were once again looking for a new coach. They turned to Alan Davies, then in charge at Nottingham. He was very highly regarded in England and was working his way up the coaching ladder at the RFU, but he was Welsh by background coming from Ynysybwl. He was supported by an East/West balance in the highly respected pair of Cardiff's Bob Norster as team manager and Llanelli's Gareth Jenkins as forwards coach.

At the start of that World Cup we lost 16–13 to Western Samoa at the National Stadium and had to put up with the jokes about the possible score line if we had played the whole of Samoa. I played a part in our try by left wing Arthur Emyr, but they tackled us out of the game and we were always behind. Alan did make a huge difference in a short time, but that World Cup was another disappointment. There was not enough preparation time, we had lost players to Rugby League, we were up against good sides. Alan decided to play Mark Ring outside half coming back from a knee injury, which may have been a gamble. I don't think Ringo had a bad game, he helped make the try for Arthur for example, but he was not 100% fit.

We were ambushed in that game. Never mind Western Samoa or the whole of Samoa, if you look at their side we were playing a lot of New Zealanders who were very, very good. Apollo Perelini and Pat Lam were great players in the back row, they had a big front five, Stephen Bachop at outside half with Frank Bunce in the centre and Brian Lima on the wing. These players became star names over the years, making a big impression in New Zealand and the northern hemisphere. Frank Bunce went on to get 55 caps for the All Blacks, for example, Pat Lam led Northampton to win the Heineken Cup.

However, I still think Robert Jones got to the ball first over the line to deny them a try which was given – so I think we should have won the game really! The sadness for me was that we were getting better as a team, but losing that first game made it difficult. We beat Argentina in midweek and then were stuffed by Australia the following weekend, without getting our hands on the ball. We failed to get out of our pool into the quarter-finals of a World Cup for the first time, but not the last. The feeling in the Holiday Inn in Cardiff that Sunday night was just horrible. Then you have to wake up to the press, they were pretty brutal and rightly so.

Once it was over, you just packed your backs and went home straightaway. The World Cup continued on our doorstep, but we were meant to return to normal. I remember just hiding away. The following weekend I was in a Cardiff team travelling to Cambridge to play while Samoa were facing Scotland in the quarter-finals, the game we should have been playing. We were listening to the build-up on the bus, thinking that should be us. It was a massive, massive disappointment, but we had the feeling we could get better in the future under new coach Alan Davies.

Alan had the problem of working with his employers at the WRU, who were trying to keep the game amateur. Sadly Alan had the job as Wales coach before his time, if he had been working in England I am sure he would still be involved in rugby somewhere because he was a visionary. He was treated quite badly at the end, but I suppose as a coach or manager you are either going to get sacked or quit at some time. He had a lot of new ideas. He was at loggerheads with Vernon Pugh for a while because he wanted to make the game more professional, get more money for the top players. The WRU were staunch defenders of amateurism, they did not know any better I suppose.

You had ridiculous things like the committee sat at the front of the plane ordering champagne on the way to away internationals, while the players sat at the back. You would have an open bar for the whole period you were in Edinburgh, or London or Dublin for the committee to get their noses in the trough, while the players would be charged for tea or coffee in their room. That attitude contributed to boys going to Rugby League, the atmosphere was not very good.

Everyone was desperate to play for Wales, it was the be all and end all for a rugby player in Wales to pull on that red jersey, but it became a bit individualistic – you were looking after your own performance to get picked for the next game rather than thinking about the team. Alan Davies changed that, the first time he picked a squad he said it would be harder to get out of the squad than it would be to get in. That led to a settled squad and a much better atmosphere.

Changing the coach just before the World Cup did not help and of course that was not a lesson which was learned. We had some poor results with the odd flicker of success in the first couple of years under Alan Davies and by 1993 he was under massive pressure. Typically everyone was focusing on the coach rather than the system.

Once again there was a huge build-up to the England game that year. We had lost in Cardiff to England in 1991 for the first time since 1963, I'd missed the game with a hamstring injury and then we had lost 24–0 in Twickenham in 1992. They were a very good side who had enjoyed Grand Slam success in 1991 and 1992 as well as reaching the World Cup Final in 1991. They were going for the title again in 1993. In contrast we were struggling because of all the players who had gone to Rugby League, as well as the other problems there were in Welsh rugby.

I watched the 1993 game against England again recently,

I could not believe how slow the game was. I also could not believe how much we were absolutely hammered, we hardly had any ball and any we did get was slow. Ieuan scored that fantastic try after Emyr Lewis's cheeky little chip. Again it was Rory Underwood and Jon Webb at wing and full back who did not spot the danger quickly enough and allowed Ieuan to nip in, kick ahead and win the chase to the line. The atmosphere in the stadium, the desperation of wanting to beat England was just like 1989. It was great to have won the game against that England, such a good side as they were at the time, but we did not play any rugby that day – it was just backs to the wall stuff. There were a couple of last ditch tackles from Mike Rayer at full back that saved us – just.

It was also notable because the England players did not come to the dinner after the game. Jerry Guscott was the only one who came. He said he had sat next to me often enough when they had won, so when we had beaten them he was not going to go missing! The rest of them went for a curry in north Cardiff somewhere, bizarre behaviour.

We were struggling at that time, players going to Rugby League, tearing ourselves apart over whether we should have leagues or no leagues, going through the same old thing. We won that game in 1993 and then used that to go on a bit of a run in 1994, we were a decent international side then. Apart from that it was just one-off victories.

1994 was obviously the best season under Alan Davies when we won the Championship. He had created a spirit and camaraderie in the Welsh team that went beyond the tribalism, the Neath, Cardiff, Llanelli, Swansea, and so on, rivalries. You were sitting in the changing room with players you had got used to literally hating. The tribalism in Welsh rugby was about hatred, but you needed someone at a Wales level who could put that aside. He got the players together and they were playing for him – and playing some pretty good rugby as well, I think. Maybe it helped that he had come from England rather than any one of those clubs.

Again we were undermined by Rugby League. Scott Gibbs was one of the stars for the Lions in New Zealand in 1993, but he went to St Helens at the start of 1994. Scott Quinnell made his Five Nations debut in 1994 and had a tremendous impact, but he too had gone to Rugby League by the end of that year. However in the 1994 Five Nations you had the feeling that Alan Davies had put his handprint on the side. Scott Quinnell was inspired in a couple of games, behind the scrum Neil Jenkins was playing really well and landing all the kicks, Ieuan Evans and Nigel Walker were try-scoring wings, while Nigel Davies settled into the inside centre role – a very different player to Scott Gibbs, he became pivotal to the way we played and the way we ran things.

The Welsh Brewers Rugby Annual for Wales said of that season: 'The pairing of the vision of Davies and the power of Mike Hall in the centre blossomed as the season progressed, Hall going on to enjoy the best season of his career. It was a Hall break that produced the crucial score in Dublin.' We could not have done anything without the ball. There were some good forwards, Mark Perego and Emyr Lewis with Scott in the back row, Gareth Llewellyn and Phil Davies in the second row, Ricky Evans, Garin Jenkins and John Davies in the front row.

We started with a 29–6 win at home to Scotland, complete with Gavin Hastings, Gregor Townsend, Kenny Milne, and my old Cambridge teammate Rob Wainwright. *Wales on Sunday* described it as Wales's best win for 15 years, making comparisons between our scoreline and the Golden Era of the 70s no less! We scored three tries, replacement wing Mike Rayer getting two and Ieuan Evans getting the third on the other wing. We beat Ireland 17–15 in Dublin and then saw off France 24–15 in Cardiff, with Scott Quinnell scoring a fantastic individual try down the right hand touchline, he made a second try scored by Nigel Walker.

We played Neath on the weekend between two of the Five Nations games. Nowadays the international players do not play any other rugby during the Six Nations, but even then

I was quite vocal asking why we were playing Neath on the Saturday before an international, knocking lumps out of each other seven days before playing alongside each other. It was just crazy. However I remember being on the floor in that game at the Arms Park and Neath and Wales prop John Davies helped me up out of harm's way. He said he did not want me to get injured because we were playing a big game the next week. That was a complete sea change in attitude, a couple of years before John and his Neath pack would have kicked the crap out of me. Alan Davies did create a Club Wales culture then and 1994 was definitely our best season, it was such a shame we could not complete the job in the final game when we went to Twickenham.

England were a good side, so to go to Twickenham and win at all is difficult, never mind when you are going for a Grand Slam and Triple Crown. That is why I admire what the current Wales team have done in the last few years by winning there twice. Winning in Twickenham was always the key to a Triple Crown or Grand Slam because it would set up the rest of the fixtures. In 1988 we won the Triple Crown because we won in Twickenham. I do not know if we went into that game in 1994 really, really believing we would beat them, they had the likes of Martin Johnson and Dean Richards leading the way up front and were very tough. There was always a question mark in the changing room at the time whenever we played the top, top teams – England, Australia, South Africa or New Zealand – as to whether we really believed we could win, arguably the same problem Wales have now.

England had lost 13–12 at home to an Ireland side inspired by wing Simon Geoghegan that season. As a result they could not win the Triple Crown or Grand Slam, but thanks to narrow wins over Scotland and France they could still win the Championship by beating us by more than 15 points. We lost the game 15–8, but narrowly enough to claim the Six Nations title on points difference. We were 16 points ahead of England overall, having scored seven tries through the Five Nations season to their two, our points difference helped largely by the scale of that win over Scotland. It was a strange feeling collecting the trophy after defeat, but once that odd moment was gone we felt we deserved it over the season.

At the end of 1994 South Africa toured for the first time since 1970, I played against them three times including consecutive Saturdays for Wales and then the Barbarians over in Dublin. Also Cardiff had played them in the opening game of the tour. It was interesting to compare the approach of the three teams against the same top class opponents.

It was funny, but sometimes I felt there was more belief in the Cardiff dressing room than there was in the Wales dressing room when we played against the top sides at that time. There was more solidity about the structures under people like Alec Evans and Terry Holmes. I believe more that Cardiff should have beaten South Africa on that tour than Wales. I think we would have if full back Mike Rayer had not got injured the week before that game. In the end we went down 11–6, but it was a really close encounter. In the Wales game against South Africa, I do not think people believed as strongly that we could win. We ended up losing 20–12 without really threatening a victory. I went from Cardiff v South Africa when we really believed we could win that game, Wales where we had a certain fragility, to the following week with the Barbarians with a bunch of southern hemisphere and English players there who knew we had a good chance. There was a debate over whether Cardiff should allow me to play in that game, as we were going well at the time and had a big game in Wales. However coach Alec Evans felt opportunities like that do not come around very often and that I should be allowed to play for the Barbarians.

It was the final game of the tour and South Africa were unbeaten. Their closest games had been Cardiff, Neath, Pontypridd and Scotland A, but they had beaten Llanelli easily and put 78 points on Swansea. They had beaten Scotland comfortably as well as Wales. However the Barbarians beat them 23–15 in that final game in Dublin, it was a really good performance to be a part of. Australian Pat Howard came off the bench when Scott Hastings got injured, he played very well at inside centre and it was good fun playing outside him. It was three different mind sets in three weeks and that was something that let us down in the Welsh game at the time, it was one of the problems.

We did not build in 1995, we lost Scott Quinnell to Rugby League and there were a lot of injuries. Then I retired from international rugby after the 1995 World Cup at the age of 29. I had enough. I took our defeats and our performances in the 1995 World Cup very personally, the fact we had not at least got to the quarter-finals. I felt I had had enough of international Rugby Union, I was going to do Rugby League instead. I went straight on holiday and should have reflected on it instead of making an immediate announcement. I should have played for a couple of months and seen how it was going, because I felt the two seasons after retiring from international rugby were my best for Cardiff – our coach Terry Holmes told me that was well.

You act in haste and repent at leisure, they say, and that applied to me in this case. They asked me to captain the side in South Africa at the start of the next season, under Alec as coach, but I declined. Then Kevin Bowring came in with completely different ideas so who knows what would have happened, I might have been dropped anyway. Allan Bateman, Scott Gibbs and others came back from Rugby League as well so competition would have been harder – but that was not a reason for retiring, I felt there was no question I was playing well enough the following season to get in.

Mentally the whole thing drained me, you have to be up for the challenge. It was probably a bad decision. I did get picked in a squad after that, for the Fiji game that autumn, but had my cheekbone broken in Llanelli so I did not figure after that.

I can reflect on 42 caps where we had some humbling defeats, but a few great highs as well. Simply playing for your country was every kid's dream. Playing under Alan Davies had some massive highs in 1993 and 1994 when we strung some wins together. Breaking into the side in 1988/9 was great, beating England a couple of times in Cardiff were great occasions. I was lucky to go to the South Seas, Canada, New Zealand, Australia, South Africa – some of the places you got to see were real experiences, remember we were amateur players at the time so that was the perk.

I would have loved to have played now when you do not have the distraction of having to work and earn a living. I had to give up a job to go on tour, that is unthinkable now, but there were certainly lots of highs to go with the lows.

11

Cardiff Rugby – from relegation to the Heineken Cup Final

WHEN LEAGUES FIRST came in to Welsh rugby in 1991, Cardiff would have been relegated from the top division that year if we had not been protected from the drop. It was quite a journey over the following few years to turn the club round to reach the top of the Welsh game and challenge strongly in Europe.

That first season of leagues was a desperate season for Cardiff. We had two protagonists, coach Alan Phillips and John Scott as team manager, who did not see things the same way and players were caught in one camp or the other. There was no real direction at the club at the time and it was floundering, a good example that historically there may have been an old fashioned way of doing things that had worked, but rugby was changing. Cardiff as a club probably did not like the idea of leagues – the idea of Cardiff being relegated was a complete no-no – they liked the status quo, they were a sleepy club with plenty of money washing around.

Both Phillips and Scott resigned and Cardiff were bold in their replacement. They went to Australia and selected someone who was not particularly well known here, but was highly respected Down Under – former Queensland and Australia forwards coach Alec Evans. He was assistant coach for Australia from 1984, when they emerged as a world power, through to 1987. He had also played a major part in turning round the fortunes of his home province Queensland. In some ways he was a nearly man – as captain of Queensland he was on the verge of playing for the Wallabies when he contracted hepatitis on a tour of New Zealand, then in 1990 he tied with Bob Dwyer in the appointment of the next Australia coach only to lose out on second ballot votes.

He may not have been well known, but when he arrived in Cardiff for the start of the 1992/3 season he absolutely shook the place to its roots. We benefitted from his Australian practices and ideas, we were successful from 1992/3 through to '97. It was his training, fitness, diet and skills which made us successful. There is no question we were one of the top two or three teams in Wales over that period and Welsh standard bearers in Europe.

When Alec arrived first of all he had been very ill with a serious blood disorder – and he looked it. We met this guy who looked terrible, but the moment I met him we struck up a rapport and I understood what he was trying to do. At the time there was a really big group of players in Cardiff who were open to what he was doing because it was different and it was new. I remember the first pre-season training we did with him which was hard, but we did no running without the ball. We were used to pre-season being running until you were sick. Alec had us doing grids, 100m long but everything was done with the ball, contacts and skills. I remember asking him when we were going to do the pre-season fitness; he looked at me as though I was some kind of idiot. Then he got his notebooks out and told me how far we had run in the last four weeks – but it had all been with the ball. It was an exciting time.

I was made captain in '93 which was also a bit controversial because I was the first Cardiff captain who was not voted in by the other players, Alec just made his choice and never mind the tradition. That put fellow Cardiff and Wales centre Mark Ring's nose out of joint because I think he thought it was his turn to be captain and he would have won the players vote. He was a wonderful player and a Cardiff boy through and through, whereas I had come in from Bridgend via Cambridge, but Alec did not care about things like that. Ringo left not long after that and went to Pontypool where he had some success playing outside half.

There was a strong spine to that team, Mike Rayer, Adrian Davies, Andy Moore, Andy Booth, Hemi Taylor, Owain Williams, Mike Griffiths. We had Simon Hill and Steve Ford on the wings, we had a mix of Cardiff boys and people from outside. Alec did not care where people came from, they were all just Cardiff players to him.

Cardiff were so traditional in the way they did things and had the big committee which Alec and I had to report to as coach and captain. We would go in and used to lose the vote 11–2 on just about everything, every time. Everything we wanted to do would be a battle. In one pre-season he said he wanted a training session on the Arms Park and then a barbecue for all the families on the pitch. I thought he had no chance, the groundsman would not let us use the pitch and getting all the families there seemed odd and different. He did it though and of course it all worked. From then on the team spirit and camaraderie in the club was strong. He had a wonderful way of doing things, much like Malky Mackay as manager at Cardiff City. That attitude from the man at the top endears people to them and there are so many instances of how he got the players on board with him. He used to have either the backs or the forwards for dinner at his house the evening before a game, just talking about anything. It was a unique way of building team spirit.

A good example of his man management was when we played Neath at the Arms Park. Their prop Brian Williams had split the eye of our second row Stuart Roy badly. Stuart was coming out of the dressing rooms after the game and his face was pretty mangled. He was about to get into his car when Alec was walking with me through the car park. He asked Stuart where he was going. He replied he was going to Cambridge, where he was a medical student, because he had an exam the next day. Alec just gave his bag to his wife Kay, got in the car and drove Stuart to Cambridge without a second thought. He booked into a hotel and brought him back after the exam the next day. Not many people do that, Cambridge is a long way but for Alec being used to the Australian outback it was nothing.

He did things for people on all sorts of different levels. For instance, when my girlfriend was very seriously ill, Alec and Kay were very supportive. Kay would go round on a Saturday afternoon and sit with her while I went off and played. Alec would help to get money for some players who were struggling for work, he would help everybody from the tea lady to the chairman. I see big similarities between Alec and Malky in the way they do that. People like that are rare.

Cardiff were a good side in that period. We won the Cup in 1994, which we had not done since 1987. We beat Llanelli 15–8, I scored a try but it was a great effort by the forwards that contained the Scarlets. We came fourth in the league that year, then we won the league in 1995 which was a tough campaign. Pontypridd were second with Treorchy third. We had the title effectively won before the last game against Newport – Pontypridd could draw level on points at the top of the table if we lost and they won, but we had a huge advantage in tries scored. It meant the trophy was at the Arms Park ready to be presented at the end of the final game against derby rivals Newport. With the title all but won, Alec rested a load of players to protect us from injury a month before the World Cup. That caused a lot of mutters because it was against Newport. The Welsh Brewers Rugby Annual for that year noted: 'Coach Alex Evans did not seem to appreciate the historic significance of Cardiff-Newport matches. Cardiff supporters were aghast at Evans' decision. Although Cardiff became league champs it was an anti-climax – and, most felt, totally unwarranted.' We lost 24–20 to make matters worse, but Treorchy beat Pontypridd so we still finished two points clear at the top.

We lost to Swansea in extra-time in the Cup semi-final that year. Then we would have won the league again in 1996, but for the introduction of bonus points for three, five and seven tries. We won one more game than Neath, but they had more bonus points. Our final games were both shown live on TV on two different channels, so it was quite an occasion. We had to score 13 tries against Llanelli – we did score 11 but it was not enough as Neath beat Pontypridd and scored seven tries for the bonus points. It was an exciting finale to the league season, though, and exciting to be a part of.

There were four or five years when I believe we were the best side in Wales. Others will disagree, but overall I think we were. Llanelli were very good, Neath, Swansea and Pontypridd were all up there, and for me that was the best period for Welsh rugby because it was full of very competitive club games. We were playing in front of full houses, against Swansea, or Bath, or whoever, the Arms Park was regularly rammed and the club game was flourishing.

It was not all easy under Alec though, the best example being the Swalec Cup loss to local Cardiff club side St Peter's in 1993. We had beaten Plymouth by 100 points the week before and they had put an extra slot on the scoreboard for three figures in preparation for the St Peter's game. The press got hold of that and had some fun. However we were playing Pontypridd in the league the Tuesday night after the Cup game, so Alec picked a side that was basically second teamers and me. I always try to say I did not play, but unfortunately I scored our try so I'm in the record books. It was not a bad side and certainly should have been good enough to win. St Peter's were a feeder club in Cardiff, but that David v Goliath feel of the early rounds of the cup certainly inspired them. St Peter's were good that day, they saw the team we put on the park and they went after us.

We went behind and struggled to get any rhythm to come back. We brought a couple of boys off the bench late in that game, Adrian Davies made an immediate difference at outside half so we still should have won it, but we didn't. After the game Alec grabbed hold of me and told me in no uncertain terms, he used to swear a lot, to front up. I went into their changing room to say well done, good luck in the next round – you can imagine the cheers and derision as you walk out of the opposition dressing room after that. As I came out I saw Alec's car going up the ramp of the Arms Park as he headed home, so much for fronting up!

We trained then the following day on the Sunday and there was pretty low feeling ahead of going to Ponty on the Tuesday. However we got it out of our system that we had lost and went up to Ponty and got the win, 6–3, in rotten conditions, which was a critical result for us at the time. That was a really good period with Alec and he has remained friends with a lot of the boys until this day. He is still involved with Queensland – he just loves rugby so much.

We spent years making Cardiff a team you love to hate. You hate us anyway, so hate us a bit more because we are going to beat you. We had a few players who could look after themselves, Hemi Taylor, Owain Williams, Tony Rees, Mike Griffiths while Dai Young came back from Rugby League, so we were not the soft touch everyone wanted us to be. We had a lot of skilful players behind the scrum as well, Nigel Walker, Andy Moore, Adrian Davies, Mark Ring for a while, and Mike Rayer, so we had a really strong side and we circled the wagons – you don't like us, bring it on.

The tribalism in Welsh rugby was about hatred. When we went to Pontypridd we knew they hated us, when we went to Llanelli we knew they hated us. I remember Alex telling us in Stradey Park he wanted us booed off – and we were. We had Tony Rees sent off, we were down to 14 men and somehow snatched a draw. It had taken us a long time to get the measure of Neath, for instance. They beat us regularly before Alec arrived, especially at their Gnoll fortress, but once we got the measure of them we beat them consistently.

My biggest regret at club level is that we did not win the Heineken Cup to be crowned kings of Europe when we should have. We reached the first final in 1996. Rugby had just gone professional and everyone was feeling their way. The Heineken

Cup was new at the start of the 1995 season and put together in a rush after the decision in August for the game to go open. The English clubs did not play in that first year, but with Vernon Pugh leading the way as chairman of the IRB they decided to plough on with the competition anyway. No-one knew how it was going to work out, but we were at the beginning of something big.

We were really excited about Europe as a team, we realised this was a huge opportunity, something different. Our first game was down in Begles-Bordeaux in France and we got a very creditable draw there. We hammered Ulster at home and smashed Leinster in Lansdowne Road in a memorable semi-final win. The Irish provinces were considered fairly easy pickings in those days, which has turned round a fair bit as they have gone from strength to strength in Europe.

With Vernon's influence and determination to get the tournament off the ground, that first final was played in January at the National Stadium in Cardiff in front of a crowd of 21,800 against French stars Toulouse – the glamour team of European rugby with players such as Thomas Castaignède and Émile Ntamack. We started badly, but then came back into the game. The match went into extra time and to this day I think the referee bottled it at the end. He gave a penalty for offside at a ruck against Wales prop Andrew Lewis, he will tell you he was on his feet and not offside. There is no way that was a penalty, but the rest is history as we lost 21–18. No Welsh side has won it and they certainly do not look like winning it now.

We were aware it was going to be something big, even though the English teams were not in it until the following season. That became our focus then, we reached a semi-final in Brives and a quarter-final in Bath the next two years. In Brives we had hooker Jonathan Humphreys sent off unluckily for a couple of technical offences, but still did better against them than Leicester managed in the final on neutral territory back in Cardiff. We let some players go, we should never have let Mike Rayer go to Bedford, we let the half-backs Andy Moore and Adrian Davies go to Richmond, it changed the whole dynamic of the side. If we had added to that side instead then I believe we could have won the Heineken Cup. We were right up there at that time challenging among the best in Europe, but we slipped away because of finances and some bad decisions by management.

The traditional strength of Welsh club rugby was beginning to slip in the professional era. Whereas once players had gone to Rugby League, now there was an exodus to English rugby clubs. Of course that offered the best of both worlds as there was a Rugby League level of money on offer and you could still play for Wales.

We had the chance to join the English leagues when Cardiff and Swansea had that rebel season in 1998/9. We had finished as the top two teams in the league the season before and we broke away for a season of friendlies with the English clubs rather than stay in Wales. I played a few of the games but had some injury problems. The first half of the season saw some great games, before the politics kicked in. We had a chance to get two teams in the English league, which I think we should have done – missing out was a big mistake. It was two franchises, going back to what Packer wanted to do, playing in the English leagues and that was our one chance. We retrenched back into ourselves in Wales and we can see the mess now.

I retired from rugby in 1999. I believe it was a mistake not keeping Terry Holmes as coach of Cardiff after Alec had finished at the end of the 1997/8 season. Terry could have been a world class coach, as good a coach as he was a player which is saying something. They got rid of Terry at the wrong time at Cardiff, he had been on a steep learning curve as assistant to Alec. He had all the attributes, he knew the game backwards and he was a hard nosed so and so. He told me after 10 years at Cardiff that he was not offering me another contract and at 34 it was time for the club to move on. I understood that, but he had no compunction about doing it which I liked about him.

Instead of keeping Terry, they brought in Lynn Howells from Pontypridd.

My 11 years at Cardiff was certainly an exciting and wonderful period to be a part of as a player and captain. It included dragging the club back from the brink of disaster, bringing in the professional era and rebuilding the image of the club. Everything has changed now with the regions taking over a few years after I retired and Cardiff Blues taking on the mantle of challenging at the top level. It would be great to see Cardiff Blues challenging in Europe on a regular basis in the way we did, but they have a long way to go. Sadly I do not see it happening unless there is a complete change of direction.

Instead everyone is bogged down by arguments. It really is appalling. Whichever side you look at, the fact it has become so personal is over the top. When they step back in a year or two they might realise the damage they have done for a generation of rugby players. It needs someone to step back and realise it is our national game, rubbishing each other in the press, making demands and counter demands while a generation of kids are getting switched off from the game is not the answer. I do not read what either side has to say any more, they just need to sort it out.

Whether Roger Lewis is a good chief executive or not, whether the regions have got a grievance or not, the longer it drags on we see ever more players disappear overseas. If I was a top player now I would go to France in a heartbeat. It is difficult enough for a small country like Wales, even if the Union and regions were fully aligned, to get themselves into a position to challenge in the top European competitions. When you add the infighting and the petty politics, you just wonder what they must think of us around the world. Someone needs to just stand up and say 'This has got to stop, it has gone too far.' There are a current generation of investors who are getting older and will pull out one day. What will happen then?

Regional rugby may have helped the Wales team flourish, but it has not worked for the regions themselves and we have lost what used to make Welsh club rugby so good. If I was running Cardiff Blues now I would drop the Blues name and just go back to being Cardiff. I would say to everybody that we are the capital city club. If they do not like that in Pontypridd then so what, they do not like the Blues either so what is there to lose?

We need to get back to our traditions of rugby – and quickly. We need the WRU and the regions as one going forward. It is hard enough for us to compete anyway at the top level of European or world rugby; we have no chance unless we are united.

12

Charity Fundraiser and TV Pundit

PEOPLE KNOW THAT Paul Guy and I invested in Cardiff City football club, we have done well generally in business, so partly this book is a chance to explain the role of the many people who helped the Cardiff City Stadium happen against the odds. There has been so much rumour that it is nice to get the opportunity to put the record straight.

However there is another side to doing the book with the decision to donate the proceeds to a deserving charity. That is also a great opportunity and hopefully will make them a little bit of much needed money as well. I have been involved in raising money for the Stepping Stones cancer charity based at Velindre Hospital in Cardiff.

There have been three big fundraising efforts so far, climbing Kilimanjaro, a bike ride from Yosemite to San Francisco in the US and also from Boston to New York. Between the three expeditions – and the fantastic efforts of an awful lot of people – we should raise comfortably over a million pounds for the charities. That is wonderful to be a part of.

We did what was called The Captains Climb of Kilimanjaro in 2011. I was one of 15 former rugby captains of Wales who did the climb, along with the likes of Ieuan Evans, Bob Norster, Eddie Butler, Rob Howley, Robert Jones, Michael Owen and Jonathan Humphreys. There were plenty of other Welsh rugby players on the trip such as Scott Gibbs, Emyr Lewis, Garin Jenkins and former Swansea and Wales lock Andy Moore. Wales and Lions coach Warren Gatland came as well, so did my business partner Paul Guy.

It was the idea of Welsh rugby photographer Huw Evans, well known to all the players, whose wife Sue was suffering from cancer. Sadly she has since died and everyone who went on that trip would want to send their best wishes to Huw and his family. He wanted to get 15 former Wales captains signed up and I was keen to do it as soon as I was approached. Huw put an incredible amount of work into making it happen and the result was a remarkable experience for everyone involved – as well as raising more that £300,000 for the Stepping Stones charity. Some of the doctors and medics from Velindre came and they were able to tell us directly where the money was going and how they were going to spend it on a new gene pool research in Velindre.

Kilimanjaro was an amazing experience. Every captain, interviewed afterwards, said it was the hardest thing they have ever done. Everyone, and Warren Gatland said the same. If you asked most of them if they would do it again, they would say no. The thing about Kilimanjaro is that it gets dark about five o'clock, you are exhausted, you have one basin of water to wash in, eating in the tent with a lamp on, the food got progressively worse as you went up even though we had over 200 natives helping to carry it up the mountain for us. It was mentally tough as well and then there was the last day in particular.

There were a lot of personalities and people who were well known on that trip, but when you are sat on the mountain peeing in a pot in a tent at 5am it does not matter who you are. Everyone had the same goal, to get to the top. Some made it, some didn't. The final couple of days are brutal, physically and mentally exhausting.

We walked across the saddle near the top of Kilimanjaro on the Sunday, got there about 2pm and you are supposed to rest in your tent until 10 or 11 at night. How can anyone get to sleep in that situation? You get up for dinner and then set off around midnight with lamps on. You get to the peaks seven or eight hours later and the return doesn't take much less, so it is pretty tough.

A few did not get there, Andy Moore turned back because his mate was not feeling well, Robert Jones didn't get there, Garin Jenkins was told by the doctors to turn back because he was suffering badly but ignored them and carried on. The Acute Mountain Sickness made it a bit of a lottery who got there and who did not, everyone was fit enough but there was more to it than that. Typically fewer than half of climbers make it all the way to the top, which is called Uhuru Peak. The last day or so is a very dangerous experience in the thin air of high altitude, you are at 19,000 feet and people can die at that altitude. Most of our party got to the rim of the volcano at a place called Gilman's Point, but there is only one 'top' on a mountain. You have to walk another hour or more to get the last 300 metres up to Uhuru Peak, which is far, far more difficult than it sounds because of the altitude.

I remember Scott Gibbs and I were hugging and crying like kids when we reached the top. It was very emotional, because it is hard work and many people are doing it for very personal reasons. The sense of fulfilling the goal is overwhelming. Then you come all the way back down, have something to eat at the base camp and then go again. When we got back down to the bottom all the people on the trip were exhausted, absolutely exhausted.

There were two particular moments which amused me. Ieuan Evans and Bob Norster were sharing a tent and you could hear Bob begging for one of these pots to pee in, Ieuan gave it to him in the end. When they woke up in the morning they found it had been kicked over in the night. Then on the afternoon and evening before we did the final day, Warren Gatland and Rob Howley's tent was right behind me and my mate Richard Crane. They did not stop talking, clearly nervous, but just hearing these two wittering away in a tent in the middle of nowhere was hilarious. Maybe they were making the plans for Wales's Grand Slam a few months later.

If Kilimanjaro was incredibly tough, so was the Yosemite to San Francisco bike ride, but in a different way. When you are riding a bike, you cannot talk too much because you are on busy roads and cannot just relax and chat. On Kilimanjaro, being able to chat was the great part of it. A lot of the walking is pretty gentle, especially early on. I walked with Warren for an afternoon and got to talk rugby with him, about his career, the way he thinks about the game, so it was fascinating. I enjoyed his company and spending time with Rob Howley as well. I was so pleased for Rob that he won the Six Nations title in 2013 as stand-in Wales coach while Warren was preparing for the Lions tour, especially after the first game when they lost to Ireland in Cardiff because he was under a lot of pressure. Rob's dedication and the way he has conducted his career is pretty spectacular, he was a professional in approach before anyone else was professional as a player – he was so fit, so good and had to battle so hard to get into that Wales team. When he got there he showed everybody what he could do.

I was on the phone for hours to try and get him to Cardiff the first time under Alec Evans. We got him there and it just did not feel right, also we had Andy Moore and Andy Booth who did not make it easy breathing down his neck. He went back to Bridgend for a couple of years, but then the second time he came to Cardiff he was absolutely magnificent. I remember in particular two tries he scored from inside our half against Llanelli in a Cup semi-final in Swansea, he was doing stuff other players could only dream of and it was great to have him in the side. He has brought all that dedication and determination to his coaching and he is pretty switched on. I think he has a really interesting coaching career future in rugby.

Kilimanjaro was tough but a great experience, we had a laugh when we got back as well. California was a different level of enjoyment, though, really good fun. Jonathan Davies is the president of Velindre and a wonderful figurehead for the charity, but he could not go to Kilimanjaro because of his broadcast commitments. He came to California a year later, as did former players Martyn Williams, Tom Shanklin, Swansea's

Andy Moore, Andy Booth and Rhys Williams. Jonathan was fantastic on that trip. There were 50 of us and he led it, he went round the campfire at night firing people up to keep going. The scenery from Yosemite down through to San Francisco, through Marin County to come to the Golden Gate Bridge, was something else. It is good fun, good charities and good people. Hopefully this book will add to those efforts – as well as setting the record straight.

While the charity fundraising has been a great thing to be involved in and keeps me in contact with some of the friends I have made through rugby, I have also been lucky enough to remain involved in the game as a TV pundit on BBC Wales. I enjoyed it while I was doing it, but every pundit has a shelf life unless you are someone like Jonathan Davies who obviously knows the game inside out and has made a great career out of it. I really enjoyed working with Eddie Butler who brought so much personality to it. He was happy to throw himself into the middle of the politics and upset people. Gwyn Jones is also a very sharp observer of the game, very intelligent and very perceptive. Now you have people like Martyn Williams coming through who are very good because they are still close to the game and the players.

13

Football versus Rugby

IT WAS VERY late on in the Cardiff City Stadium process that Cardiff council decided that they wanted Cardiff Blues rugby club to play there as well so that the effective grants they were investing could be seen to benefit more than just the football community. I think they just wanted this wonderful new stadium to benefit both major teams in Cardiff if possible.

I always thought there might be an opportunity for the Blues at the new stadium, but no-one at the football club, first Hammam and then Ridsdale, wanted to go along with that and I did not push it. However at a meeting on 3 October 2006, just under three weeks before we got Sam Hammam to resign as chairman, Cardiff council told Paul Guy and Peter Ridsdale they wished to see ground sharing with the Blues and that was now one of the conditions for going ahead with the project. Almost out of nowhere it had become a potential sticking point, just when we could see light at the end of the tunnel in terms of the problems with Hammam.

I went to see Cardiff Blues chairman Peter Thomas after the Blues had played a game and said there was a real opportunity because they could move from a dilapidated Arms Park – which it was and still is – to a brand new stadium. They could cut a deal on the rental and arrange the premium seating to provide a potentially big income to underpin the Blues and rugby in the region going forward.

Yes they would pay an annual rent for the use of the stadium, but there was greater potential for revenue through the higher gates and better hospitality facilities. If they wanted to be able to match the European giants on the pitch then they needed the support and hospitality revenue to match them off the pitch. I think Peter saw that, but sadly the stadium never worked for them because there is no support for regional rugby. There is nothing wrong with the stadium; it was the product on the pitch which did not work for rugby at the Cardiff City Stadium.

Going from Cardiff RFC to the Cardiff Blues and then moving to the bigger stadium was a chance to create the crowds and revenue they have in the Super 15 Down Under and in the English game, but it just has not worked because there is not the support for it in Wales.

I felt quite sad when Cardiff Blues decided to return to the Arms Park because Peter and chief executive Bob Norster really took a leap of faith to drag everybody with them to the Cardiff City Stadium. There were many people who did not want to leave the Arms Park – and this is coming from someone who played there for over a decade so I loved the ground and understand all that. I still think the move was a great missed opportunity for them.

The council pushed it for the good of the Blues. It became a really important part of the deal in developing the new stadium, very important in fact, in the final stages before it went through. The council saw where the Blues were at the Arms Park and thought that, rightly or wrongly, if they went to the new stadium they could go on to bigger and better things.

I don't think Peter Ridsdale ever wanted them there, he wasn't at all bothered about the Blues or rugby. He found it an irritant having to deal with them, the thought of sharing the stadium, sharing offices, all that sort of stuff was not for him. There was never a meeting of minds there. All Peter was interested in was the football and who can blame him for that. However I believe it was the only chance for the Blues to move up to the level where they could challenge the best in Europe. They will never be able to challenge Leicester or Leinster or the French clubs as long as they are based at the Arms Park, it is just too small and the facilities are not good enough.

I don't think the deal with the Cardiff City Stadium was the problem either, I think the rent was fair and they were given a clean stadium to do their own marketing and advertising. There was one simple reason it did not work and that was the product on the pitch, end of story.

It does not matter if you have the best facilities in the world, if you have drab rugby in a boring tournament it will not work. People have got out of the habit of watching live regional rugby. TV coverage has ruined the sport in some ways because there are simply too many games shown live, plus staging them on Friday and Saturday evenings to suit the TV schedules is at odds with when people want to watch live rugby. TV want to show them at that time because more people are at home, but if they are at home then they are less likely to go to a game – by definition there is a straightforward conflict between attracting a live audience and TV viewing figures. Meanwhile Cardiff City have been playing football in the Championship and then the Premiership, with most home games pretty much every other Saturday afternoon at 3pm. Football fans are in the habit of going to watch their team at a reasonably regular slot. Add to that the fact going to the football at the Cardiff City Stadium is now a great day out. The Blues lost that atmosphere, there were not enough competitive games and people got out of the habit of going.

Also you have the attitude that many are simply not interested in the regions, they do not hold the emotional attachment that brought packed houses to the club game in my playing days. The sooner we bite the bullet and admit that in rugby, the better. In ten years time we will still be saying the regions are not working. Most people living in Pontypridd do not want to travel to watch Cardiff. I do not think you will ever change that. They are up in the Valleys and do not want to support the big city team when they have been used to having their own side to support – and I respect that opinion. There was no better atmosphere than a full Sardis Road and they produced huge amounts of talent.

A lot of Cardiff City's support is from the Valleys, but it is different because there have never been more than two or three football clubs at Football League level in south Wales whereas the rugby tribalism is pretty deep-seated. We have to go back to that tribalism as soon as we can. It is about the Cardiff city-slickers going up the valley to play Ponty, it is about Swansea playing Llanelli, Bath or Gloucester coming over the bridge to play Pontypool – that is what gets the juices going. The sad thing for Peter Thomas and the rest of the people funding regional rugby is that they can do all the marketing, but some people simply will not go and support the regional team in their area.

Rugby fans made a massive amount of the mile and a half from the city centre to the Cardiff City Stadium. They had huge car parking at the new stadium, a convenient bus service to and from there, better facilities, a better pitch to play on, they had everything. There was a noisy minority of fans who liked having a pint in a particular pub in the centre of Cardiff before walking across to the Arms Park, or drinking in the Athletic Club at the Arms Park, so they kicked up a big fuss. However going back to the Arms Park has not been a panacea for all their ills. It never will be, as it puts a ceiling on what they can achieve in the future.

I used to go and watch Cardiff City and Cardiff Blues playing three or four days apart at the Cardiff City Stadium. It was a fantastic atmosphere with the football and I would take the kids who loved it. Then I would go back for the rugby, there wouldn't be anybody there to watch a drab game that wouldn't excite anybody. I would sit there and wonder how the experience could be so different, especially when I personally desperately wanted the rugby to work. When the Blues played Australia at the stadium I was hoping it would be a full house, but even then it wasn't. There were a couple of great occasions there, a big crowd and really good game against the Ospreys for instance. In the Celtic competitions there are few away fans, so that makes a difference too as there is no atmosphere.

There is a different cultural element of supporting the football. When I go away with the rugby players I played with, we talk about football now. That is what we are getting excited about. We could not wait to have the box at the Cardiff City Stadium in the Premiership – even if only for a season. Cardiff City sold out of season tickets for that season and I had people I know through rugby ringing me up asking if I could get a season ticket for them. That excitement is something we used to have in rugby.

I was fortunate to play when there were people hanging off trees watching us. That was because it was a Cardiff side that had an identity, but now not even Cardiff people identify with the Blues. There is an antipathy there, people do not know what competition is when and they are not interested. I do not know how you change that unless you do something completely radical. We had that rebel season with Cardiff and Swansea playing in England that was a chance if we had grasped it. The whole system appears fundamentally flawed to me.

Just when everyone needs to get together to work out ways of getting over all these problems, instead you have the regions and the WRU arguing about the same old things. They need to be careful because they are in danger of being swamped, all the things they are arguing over will simply not matter either way.

If Cardiff and Swansea City can be in the Premier League long term then they would be two huge businesses in Wales with turnovers of £100 million – that makes each of them far bigger than the WRU! In terms of the audiences they are reaching, live crowds, television audiences and the corporate pound, football will absolutely blow regional rugby away. If you are a big company in Wales and deciding where to do your corporate entertaining, then there is only one answer. The Cardiff City Stadium was sold out for almost every game in the

Premier League, while they still struggle to get sell-outs at the smaller Cardiff Arms Park.

When the Blues went back to the Arms Park I thought it was a massive sign of failure for the ambition and direction of rugby. For the fans to blame the stadium, which obviously I'm quite passionate about, I just thought it was all wrong. They need to look at the pitch and the facilities which are first class. You could have a totally different experience going to watch the football from the rugby. It is a massive backward step for the Blues and I don't really know how they recover from it. If you have tried to reach out to do something different to compete with the Leicester's, the Harlequins and the Leinster's, then fallen back, where do you go from there?

Peter Thomas has carried the burden there for a long time and gets a lot of unnecessary vitriol from people when he has put his cold, hard cash into the club as well as considerable time and effort. As far as I'm concerned the Union should be buying him out, making him a life member of the WRU, thanking him, putting his name on a plaque somewhere. Then they should go in and invest in the regions to take control and to revive them. You cannot think the top of the game, in terms of Wales's international results, will continue to go well if the regions are not competitive. You cannot have a non-competitive environment in the regions and expect to keep producing good players. We have some good players coming through at the moment but that cannot carry on. You need a pyramid with a strong base, so the tip is as competitive as possible.

I went back to the Arms Park two years ago for the Toulon game in the Pool stages of the Heineken Cup. Toulon went on to win it (but lost there when drawn with the Blues the following season) so obviously they were a top side, lead by Jonny Wilkinson and with international star names everywhere you looked. It is simply impossible to get more glamorous opponents in European rugby. There was a decent atmosphere for the game, but I was expecting it to be rammed. It took a long time to get a pie and pint, while in these modern stadia now it is so quick and easy and that is where you make your money. The corporate facilities were nowhere near as good at the Arms Park either. Those hospitality boxes at each end were brilliant when they were built in my playing days, but things have moved on and they are not what people expect any more.

Welsh rugby is still behaving in the way it did 20 years ago, tearing themselves apart. The difference now is that the WRU have got it right at the international level, but how long can they sustain that. They have hired the top coaches, put a huge amount of resource into it, built a fantastic training facility out at the Vale.

I think the Union should be working with the regions to create at least two sides who can compete in the Heineken Cup. To achieve that we need to fundamentally change the way we look at rugby in this country. I would even go back to the club system for the bulk of the domestic rugby season, with two to three sides that we enter in the Heineken Cup. We could arrange the season so the clubs can play against each other in the old historical ties, then have the best players going forward to a regional squad with a different coach and manager to compete in Europe.

If we carry on as we are we will have no one qualifying for the quarter-finals of Europe for many years to come. Obviously you will get the odd exception, but not a sustained assault at the final stages of the European Cup. The Ospreys have the squad to get there with a decent draw, but you need back-up players to the main players and I am not sure the Welsh regions have the depth of squad to match the best teams around.

While Cardiff City have been buying stars in for millions of pounds – Wales and Lions centre Jamie Roberts and Lions man-of-the-series Leigh Halfpenny went the other way in leaving the capital. It speaks volumes about the fortunes of the two biggest sporting teams in Cardiff.

This view will be controversial with many in Welsh rugby, but I think the WRU need to be running all the regions and that is the only way it is going to work. When you look at the money in Welsh rugby and the money running through the WRU, then it is a no-brainer. A similar approach is working well in Ireland, it has worked well in a place like Australia since the beginning of professionalism.

I would do a deal with the owners for the WRU to effectively buy them out of the regions. Those owners probably know they are not going to get all their money back, any more than if those businesses went into administration. Then I would say to those owners that we appreciate what they have all done for the regional game in Wales and make each of them a life vice-president of the WRU, they can come to any of the regional or international games whenever they want. Their contribution to Welsh rugby is recognised while the burden is taken away. That is better than sending these people off without anything, as happened when former director Mike Cuddy left the Ospreys. Then the WRU can work out how to take the regions forward.

The WRU needs to run the academies at the four regions, as it does, it needs to be able to take control of the boys coming out of those academies and where they go before they make it in the first teams, where they go to university and so on. There is a danger because those boys in the academies do not play very often. We need to keep producing players but they need to be playing. The WRU need to be running the professional game from the top to the bottom. Sadly the regions will probably need to go bankrupt before anything like that can happen, the whole thing is so personality led that common sense is in short supply.

If I was going to watch rugby now I would probably go to Harlequins or Bath. We used to be like that, full houses, great atmosphere. The English league has marketed itself so well, for example hiring Wembley and Twickenham for games, selling the tickets cheap to get people in and putting on a day of entertainment to make it worthwhile. Those are people who might then go and watch the more normal club games. We have Judgement Day with the four regions playing at the

Millennium Stadium a couple of weeks after the end of the Six Nations. It was OK and was something they can build on, but it is a terrible shame the regions and the WRU are not doing more in terms of going forward together.

I have also found there is a massive difference between rugby fans and football fans. The football fans wanted the stadium to happen in Cardiff, they embraced it, they wanted out of Ninian Park. The stadium now has become a fantastic centre-piece for the club and Cardiff City owner Vincent Tan will take it to another level. He has invested in the ambitious expansion of the stadium; all we need is Premier League football there again.

It will all be so different to when I was playing rugby for Cardiff. Then we were playing in front of full houses at Cardiff Arms Park and Cardiff City were playing in front of four or five thousand. We used to bump into some of their players in town, we almost felt sorry for them. Now it is completely different, the football guys will be in a different league in every sense.

There is a perennial argument over what is the national sport of Wales. Historically there has only been one answer to that question – rugby has been the national sport without question. Internationally rugby is seen as the national sport in Wales. It may not be the global game that football is, but Welsh success on the rugby field has been far greater than in football so it has done a lot more to get Wales known.

Now I am not so sure. Wales's club football is permanently up; this is not a flash in the pan. What Swansea in particular have done is remarkable, winning the Carling Cup and staying in the Premier League with a positive brand of football, even the most die-hard Cardiff fan has to admit that is incredible. They change managers without it seeming to change things, they attract top class players to Swansea, that is fantastic and will continue to be a great success story for Wales and Welsh sport. It is in direct comparison with the Ospreys who share the stadium.

Cardiff City football will have Vincent Tan there, certainly for the medium term. He needs to get back to the Premier League and stay there for a couple of years before he can do anything to get any of his money back or think of selling the club. That is good news for Cardiff fans because he has got the money to do it. The danger is that we could have a maverick, wealthy owner who is trying to do the right thing but does not understand football or sport. If he treats it as just another business, hires and fires at will, then we might not get anywhere for two to three years.

Cardiff and Swansea have had remarkable exposure round the world because of the football, some negative and some positive, but the coverage is enormous. Rugby can never compete with that because it is a smaller game worldwide.

Despite all the in-fighting at regional level, the signs are really good for the Wales rugby team. I am weary of the in-fighting, bored of the politics, though Wales are still successful at national level. The contribution to the Lions win in Australia showed that, with 10 Welsh players starting the final Test and arguably it could have been more. Then there is the Under 20s getting to the final of the Junior World Championships, beating South Africa in the semi-final, in 2013. I wonder how long we can sustain it without a strong regional game, but we will see. We have some fantastic players, there is no question about that.

I would love to be able to go down the Arms Park and watch top players in a meaningful game. I would like to have a similar experience there that you get at Cardiff City football. In terms of fighting for the sporting pound going forward, it is very competitive and the regions are nowhere near where they need to be. We probably have a generation who would have been brought up watching rugby but have now missed out.

Wales are still successful because they have a brilliant coach in Warren Gatland with a really good coaching team around him. They have been able to take one group of players and be successful, then when those players moved on they were able to take another group to the same success. He has a contract until

2019, but will he stay if all the politics keeps dragging things down? We are extremely lucky to have him, if we did end up with a new coach then I am not sure the current success will continue. There are too many unknowns with Welsh rugby at the moment.

The balance in Welsh sport has shifted from Welsh rugby to Welsh football. Rugby has a chance to slow that down, but it may be an uphill battle. I fear for the future of the sport I played, but I am confident about the future of the sport I ended up getting involved in through business.

That is just one of the many things that have taken me by surprise since I first started playing club rugby for Maesteg in the late 1980s. I could never have predicted the rollercoaster journey, in the end it has been a good one. The Chinese saying goes 'may you live in interesting times'. I have certainly managed that.

Also available from Y Lolfa:

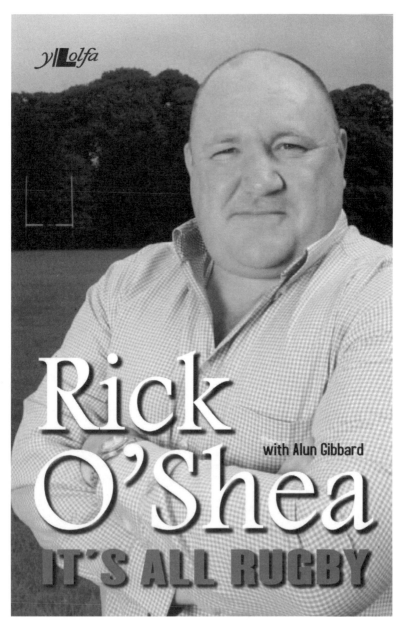

£9.95

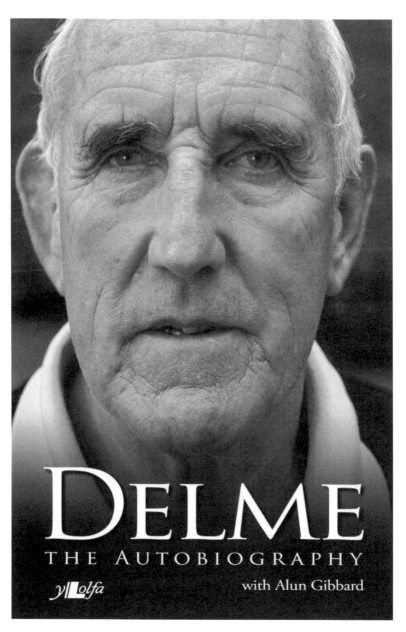

DELME

THE AUTOBIOGRAPHY

y Lolfa

with Alun Gibbard

£9.95

The Mike Hall Story is just one of a whole range of publications from Y Lolfa. For a full list of books currently in print, send now for your free copy of our new full-colour catalogue. Or simply surf into our website

www.ylolfa.com

for secure on-line ordering.

T<small>ALYBONT</small> C<small>EREDIGION</small> C<small>YMRU</small> SY24 5HE
e-mail ylolfa@ylolfa.com
website www.ylolfa.com
phone (01970) 832 304
fax 832 782